LENT WITH EVELYN UNDERHILL

LENT WITH EVELYN UNDERHILL

Selections from her writings

Second Edition

EDITED BY
G. P. MELLICK BELSHAW

MOREHOUSE PUBLISHING
Harrisburg, PA

First published in 1964 by A. R. Mowbray and Co., Ltd.

Morehouse Publishing
Harrisburg, Pennsylvania

Library of Congress Cataloging-in-Publication Data

Underhill, Evelyn. 1875-1941.
  Lent with Evelyn Underhill: selections from her writings/edited by G.P. Mellick Belshaw.—2nd ed.
    p. cm.
  Reprint, with new pref. Originally published: New York: Morehouse-Barlow, 1964.
  ISBN: 0-8192-1449-3
  1. Lent—Prayer-books and devotions—English. I. Belshaw, G.P. Mellick. II. Title.
BV85.U53   1990   89-28659
242'.34—dc20   CIP

Second Printing, 1993

Printed in the United States of America
by
BSC LITHO
Harrisburg, Pennsylvania

Preface to the Second Edition

Looking back over twenty-five years since this little book of readings from the writings of Evelyn Underhill was published, I believe her lasting achievement remains her contribution to a renewed interest in the Christian mystical tradition.

During her life the influence of the Roman Catholic lay-theologian Friedrich von Hügel was considerable. Nowhere is that clearer than in the distinction he made between exclusive and inclusive mysticism. It took time in her spiritual journey to advance from the experience of an exclusive mysticism of the kind described by the Neo-Platonist philosopher, Plotinus, as "the flight of the alone to the Alone," with its search for private religious experience, to an inclusive mysticism that emphasized community. She grew in her spiritual formation to appreciate a mysticism that included sacraments—especially the Eucharist—and which focused on the incarnation of Christ, the reality of evil, the encounter with suffering, and the institutional life of the Church.

Evelyn Underhill sprinkled her writings with appropriate quotations from the saints and mystics. She wrote from the perspective of one living in two worlds, the visible and the invisible. Consequently she regarded the human being as "amphibious"—belonging to this world here and now and the other world beyond space and time. The analogy of a house with its upper and lower stories appealed to her as expressive of the connection between earth and heaven.

Given her attraction to the mystical tradition it is understandable why she liked the analogy of a fish in the sea. The fish swims in the ocean but does not create it, neither does the Christian at prayer create the life of prayer but enters into it and is invigorated by it. For her the milieu of prayer encompassed the personal experience of the individual and the corporate experience of the Church. In all this we see the influence of von Hügel, who criticized individualistic, private, religious experience, separated from others, from community, from this world, and from the reality of evil and suffering. Those who succumbed to such spirituality von Hugel called "detached;" he dubbed them "D's!"

In Colossians 1:15 and following, Paul writes that Jesus is the "first-born of all creation," and head of the Church. Mystics have always been attracted to the Cosmic Christ of Paul's letters. That was true for Evelyn Underhill, as it was for another twentieth century mystic, Teilhard de Chardin, who would have applauded her words found in her book, *Mysticism:*

> The Incarnation, which is for popular Christianity synonymous with the historical birth and early life of Christ, is for the mystic not only this but also a perpetual cosmic and personal process. It is an everlasting bringing forth, in the universe and also in the individual ascending soul, of the divine and perfect Life, and pure character of God, of which the one historical life dramatized the essential constituents.

As I have returned to the writings of Evelyn Underhill for enrichment, there have been times when in spite of keeping in mind the historical setting in which she wrote—England just prior to World War I through the inter-war period—I have been uncomfortable with certain dualisms of thought. Her frequent use of "supernatural," God as "objective reality," priority given to adoration in prayer, her favorite two-storied house analogy, patriarchal imagery, and quaint illustrations that often seem dated can be a problem. But these troubling areas are more than compensated and usually transcended by her constant incarnational spirituality, her celebration of creation, her view of discipleship as pilgrimage and growth in Christ, her belief in worship as response to God's loving search for us, and her focus on community—in short, by her inclusive mysticism.

Drawing us into deeper levels of understanding, Evelyn Underhill's writings cultivate a contemplative approach to God and creation. With her aesthetic sensibility she writes of the presence of God everywhere, even in the most insignificant encounter or thing. And finally, in a Johannine spirit she calls us to open our eyes, to see!

It is fitting then that the liturgical calendar of the Episcopal Church now sets aside June 15 as the day to commemorate "Evelyn Underhill, Theologian and Mystic."

G. P. MELLICK BELSHAW

Introduction

I SHALL never forget an event that took place during the early days of my first term at the General Theological Seminary, New York. My faculty adviser had made an appointment with me, and I expected a discussion about my courses. The Very Rev. Cuthbert A. Simpson, now Dean of Christ Church, Oxford, but at that time Professor of Old Testament at the Seminary, was seated at his desk as I entered his study. Prepared to give an evaluation of the progress of my studies, I was utterly surprised when he looked up and said: 'How are your meditations coming along?' The brief but awkward silence which followed communicated the answer clearly. 'Well,' I answered, 'is there something that you could recommend to get me on the right tack?' He thought for a moment, and replied, 'Have you ever read anything by Evelyn Underhill? If not, why don't you try the *Mystery of Sacrifice?* It was a good choice, for in that short but profound meditation on the liturgy, I was introduced to the essence of her thought. The book opened up the whole world of her writings, the pursuit of which has proved to be a continuingly rewarding experience.

Evelyn Underhill died in 1941, and the list of books, essays, addresses, letters, and poems that she produced, beginning with the turn of the century, is remarkable. Her early book *Mysticism* remains to this day a classic in the field, and her later book *Worship,* published in 1936, is still widely read and appreciated. However, for me, she reaches her heights in some of her less ambitious undertakings—her shorter books, such as the *School of Charity* and *Concerning the Inner Life*—and particularly in her addresses given at retreats and in her letters. The latter reveal her love for, and frankness with, a series of friends and acquaintances.

Evelyn Underhill's thought developed from an early fascination with the mystical tradition in Christianity to a decidedly incarnational and sacramental point of view, but never at the expense of the positive contributions of Christian mysticism which she traced from the New Testament to the present. The Roman Catholic lay-theologian, Baron Friedrich von Hügel, played an important part in guiding her into a realization of the 'given-ness' of Christianity, especially as this is seen in the historical event of the Incarnation and the subsequent life of the institutional Church. She learned to place heavy emphasis on the doctrine of creation and the prevenience of God, so that the Christian life became for her a response to God's self-revelation rather than a human seeking after God. Her spirituality was never subjective nor shallow, and it became increasingly more dependent upon the transcendence of God and His loving search for man's obedience.

What could man's attitude be other than a humble adoration? —so thought Evelyn Underhill. As Frederick Denison Maurice, the great nineteenth-century exponent of the Anglican approach, had already written: 'The more near [the believer] is brought to God, the greater he feels the necessity for adoration and worship,' and for her this became especially real in sacramental worship. She had nothing to do with individualistic pietism, and her religion was at one with the corporate worship of the Church. Her love for and her interest in worship stimulated her to study the historic liturgies, of which she became a most competent scholar. Nevertheless, she did not stop there with a scholarly concern for worship; she went on to emphasize that the Christian life was not only seen in belief and worship, but must be fulfilled in practice. Her addresses on the fruit of the Spirit, and her love for the poor, demonstrate her conviction that the Christian 'way' of commitment is not something possessed but offered.

The following selections from the writings of Evelyn Underhill are intended to be used daily during the course of a Lenten season. Many a Christian has emphasized that far greater meaning can be extracted from Holy Scripture and devotional literature when the length of time spent in reading, rather than the number of pages read, is stressed. This holds true in the use of these selections.

Evelyn Underhill's writings are filled with meat, and they can only be appreciated and digested with time and concentration.

The selections are chosen with the purpose of deepening the reader's Lenten observance by following the thought of Evelyn Underhill, to whom many of us look as the outstanding modern Anglican writer on the 'interior life,' and whose prayer and understanding was so firmly rooted in the classical spiritual writers of the Christian Church. In order not to distract from the content of her thought, footnotes have been omitted, but each reading has been identified with reference to book, essay, or letter, in which it first appeared.

G. P. MELLICK BELSHAW

Contents

ACKNOWLEDGEMENTS

GRATEFUL acknowledgement is made to the following for permission to reprint material from books of which they hold the copyright:

LONGMANS, GREEN & CO., INC., for permission to quote from *School of Charity* by Evelyn Underhill. Copyright 1934. *Abba* by Evelyn Underhill. Copyright 1940. *Light of Christ* by Evelyn Underhill. Copyright 1945. *The Letters of Evelyn Underhill*, ed. Charles Williams. Copyright 1934. *The Mount of Purification* by Evelyn Underhill. Copyright 1960. *Collected Papers of Evelyn Underhill*, ed. Lucy Menzies. Copyright 1946. *The Mystery of Sacrifice* by Evelyn Underhill. Copyright 1938. *The Fruits of the Spirit* by Evelyn Underhill. Copyright 1942. Permission granted by DAVID MCKAY COMPANY, New York, with whom LONGMANS, GREEN & CO., INC., New York, has merged.

E. P. DUTTON & CO., INC., for permission to quote from *The Golden Sequence* by Evelyn Underhill. Copyright 1933, by E. P. DUTTON & CO., INC. Renewal 1961, by H. STUART MOORE. Reprinted by permission of the publishers. From the volume *Concerning the Inner Life* and *The House of the Soul* by Evelyn Underhill. Copyright 1930, by E. P. DUTTON & CO., INC. Renewal 1958, by H. STUART MOORE. Reprinted by permission of the publishers. From *The Mystic Way* by Evelyn Underhill. Copyright 1913. From the book *Man and the Supernatural* by Evelyn Underhill. Copyright 1928, by E. P. DUTTON & CO., INC. Renewal 1956, by H. STUART MOORE. Reprinted by permission of the publishers.

JAMES NISBET & CO., LTD., for permission to quote from *Worship* by Evelyn Underhill. Copyright 1936.

Acknowledgement is also made to JAMES CLARKE & CO., LTD., for permission to quote from *Theological Essays* by F. D. Maurice. This edition published in 1957. Thanks are due to Tom Goddard for the cover decoration.

LENT WITH EVELYN UNDERHILL

✝

In the triumph of prayer
Twofold is the spell.
With the folding of hands
There's a spreading of wings
And the soul's lifted up to invisible lands
And ineffable peace. Yet it knows, being there
That it's close to the heart of all pitiful things;
And it loses and finds, and it gives and demands;
For its life is divine, it must love, it must share
In the triumph of prayer.

From '*Theophanies*'

Ash Wednesday

A TIME FOR SELF-EXAMINATION

EVERYONE who is engaged on a great undertaking, depending on many factors for its success, knows how important it is to have a periodical stocktaking. Whether we are responsible for a business, an institution, a voyage, or an exploration—even for the well-being of a household—it is sometimes essential to call a halt; examine our stores and our equipment, be sure that all necessaries are there and in good order, and that we understand the way in which they should be used. It is no good to have tins without tin openers, bottles of which the contents have evaporated, labels written in an unknown language, or mysterious packages of which we do not know the use. Now the living-out of the spiritual life, the inner life of the Christian—the secret correspondence of his soul with God—is from one point of view a great business. It was well called 'the business of all businesses' by St. Bernard; for it is no mere addition to Christianity, but its very essence, the source of its vitality and power. From another point of view it is a great journey; a bit-by-bit progress, over roads that are often difficult and in weather that is some-times pretty bad, from 'this world to that which is to come.' Whichever way we look at it, an intelligent and respectful attitude to our equipment—seeing that it is all there, accessible and in good condition, and making sure that we know the real use of each item—is essential to its success. It is only too easy to be deluded by the modern craving for pace and immediate results, and press on without pausing to examine the quality and character of our supplies, or being sure that we know where we are going and possess the necessary maps. But this means all the disabling miseries of the unmarked route and unbalanced

14

diet; and at last, perhaps, complete loss of bearings and consequent starvation of the soul. . . .

Lent is a good moment for such a spiritual stocktaking; a pause, a retreat from life's busy surface to its solemn deeps. There we can consider our possessions; and discriminate between the necessary stores which have been issued to us, and must be treasured and kept in good order, and the odds and ends which we have accumulated for ourselves. Most of us are inclined to pay considerable attention to the spiritual odds and ends: the air-cushions, tabloids, and vacuum flasks, and various labour-saving devices which we call by such attractive names as our own peace, our own approach, our own experience, and so forth. But we leave the superb and massive standard equipment which is issued to each baptized Christian to look after itself. There are few who cannot benefit by a bit-by-bit examination of that equipment, a humble return to first principles; for there we find the map and road-book of that spiritual world which is our true environment, all the needed information about the laws which control it, and all the essentials for feeding that inner life of which we talk so much and understand so very little.

The School of Charity

First Thursday in Lent

THE SPIRITUAL LIFE: BELIEF AND PRAYER

THE spiritual life is a stern choice. It is not a consoling retreat from the difficulties of existence; but an invitation to enter fully into that difficult existence, and there apply the Charity of God and bear the cost. Till we accept this truth, religion is full of puzzles for us, and its practices often unmeaning: for we do not know what it is all about. So there are few things more bracing and enlightening than a deliberate resort to these superb statements about God, the world and the soul; testing by them our attitude to those realities, and the quality and vigour of our interior life with God. For every one of them has a direct bearing on that interior life. . . . Our prayer and belief should fit like hand and glove; they are the inside and outside of one single correspondence with God. Since the life of a prayer consists in an ever-deepening communion with a Reality beyond ourselves, which is truly there, and touches, calls, attracts us, what we believe about that Reality will rule our relation to it. We do not approach a friend and a machine in the same way. We make the first and greatest of our mistakes in religion when we begin with ourselves, our petty feelings and needs, ideas and capacities. The Creed sweeps us up past all this to God, the objective Fact, and His mysterious self-giving to us. It sets first Eternity and then History before us, as the things that truly matter in religion; and shows us a humble and adoring delight in God as the first duty of the believing soul. So there can hardly be a better inward discipline than the deliberate testing of our vague, dilute, self-occupied spirituality by this superb vision of Reality.

These great objective truths are not very fashionable among modern Christians; yet how greatly we need them, if we are to escape pettiness, individualism and emotional bias. For that mysterious inner life which glows at the heart of Christianity, which we recognize with delight whenever we meet it, and which is the source of Christian power in the world, is fed through two channels. Along one channel a certain limited knowledge of God and the things of God enters the mind; and asks of us that honest and humble thought about the mysteries of faith which is the raw material of meditation. Along the other channel God Himself comes secretly to the heart, and wakes up that desire and that sense of need which are the cause of prayer. The awestruck vision of faith and the confident movement of love are both needed, if the life of devotion is to be rich, brave and humble; equally removed from mere feeling and mere thought. Christian prayer to God must harmonize with Christian belief about God: and quickly loses humility and sanity if it gets away from that great law. We pray first because we believe something; perhaps at that stage a very crude or vague something. And with the deepening of prayer, its patient cultivation, there comes—perhaps slowly, perhaps suddenly—the enrichment and enlargement of belief, as we enter into a first-hand communion with the Reality who is the object of our faith.

The School of Charity

First Friday in Lent

THE THREE COUNSELS

EACH person's discipline, of course, will be different because what God wants from each of us is different. Some are called to an active and some to a passive life, some to very homely and some to hard and sacrificial careers, some to quiet suffering. Only the broad lines will be alike. But no discipline will be any use to us unless we keep in mind the reason why we are doing this—for the Glory of God, and not just for the sake of our own self-improvement or other self-regarding purpose. Our object is to be what God wants of us, not what we want of Him. So all that we do must be grounded in worship. First lift up our eyes to the hills, then turn to our own potato field and lightly fork in the manure.

All this suggests that though this outer discipline is very important for us, there is something deeper and more secret that God asks of us, if we really desire to give our lives to Him. Our Lord demanded great renunciation of those who wanted to follow Him. He never suggested that the Christian life was an easy or comfortable affair. The substance of what He asked is summed up in what are called the 'evangelical counsels'— Poverty, Chastity and Obedience. We know that those who enter religious communities accept these counsels in their most literal form. They do give up all their possessions, their natural and human relationships, the freedom of their wills. But in one way or another, something of their spirit is needed by everyone who really desires to follow Christ. The New Testament means what it says when it demands poverty of spirit, purity of heart and filial obedience from all who would do this. And the reason is, that each of these qualities in a different way detaches us from the unreal and self-regarding interests with which (almost without knowing it) we usually fill up our lives. They simplify us, clear the ground for God; so that our relation of utter dependence on Him stands out as the one reality of our existence. So it might be profitable for us this Lent to meditate on the three Counsels and see what light they cast on our own lives.

'Letter to the Prayer Group, Lent 1941,' *The Fruits of the Spirit*

First Saturday in Lent

THE THREE COUNSELS CONSIDERED

FIRST, think of *Poverty*. Even outward Poverty, a hard and simple life, the dropping for love's sake of the many things we feel we 'must have' is a great help in the way of the Spirit. Far more precious is that inward Poverty of which it is the sacrament; which frees us from possessions and possessiveness and does away with the clutch of 'the I, the Me and the Mine' upon our souls. We can all strive for this internal grace, this attitude of soul, and it is a very important part of the life of prayer. The Holy Spirit is called the Giver of Gifts and the Father of the Poor; but His cherishing action is only really felt by those who acknowledge their own deep poverty—who realize that we have literally nothing of our own, but are totally dependent on God and on that natural world in which God has placed us and which is the sacramental vehicle of His action. When we grasp this we are ready to receive His gifts. Some souls are so full of pious furniture and ornaments, that there is no room for Him. All the correct things have been crammed into the poor little villa, but none of the best quality. They need to pull down the curtains, get rid of the knick-knacks, and throw their premises open to the great simplicity of God. . . .

Chastity. The counsel of Chastity does not, of course, mean giving up marriage but something much more subtle and penetrating. It really means the spirit of poverty applied to our emotional life—all the clutch and feverishness of desire, the 'I want' and 'I must have' taken away and replaced by absolute single-mindedness, purity of heart. This may involve a deliberate rationing of the time and energy we give to absorbing personal relationships with others—unnecessary meetings, talks and letters—to special tastes and interests, or, worst of all, self-occupied daydreams and broodings about ourselves, cravings for sympathy and interest. We have to be very firm with ourselves about all this, making war on every kind of possessiveness, self-centredness, and clutch. From all these entanglements Christ's spirit of chaste Love will set us free; for it is a selfless, all embracing charity—friendship with God, and with all His creatures for His sake. . . .

Obedience. This means the total surrender of our wills, which are the greatest obstacles to our real self-giving to God. The more we get rid of self-chosen aims, however good, the more supple we are to His pressure, the nearer we get to the pattern of the Christian life, which is summed up in 'not my will but Thine be done.' Then, not before, we are ready to be used as God's tools and contribute to His purpose. Since God is the true doer of all that is done, it is always for Him to initiate and for us to respond, and this willing response is the essence of obedience. Obedience means more freedom not less, for it lifts the burden of perpetual choice, and in so doing actually increases our power of effective action by making us the instruments of God's unlimited action. When the whole Church is thus obedient to Him it will be what it is meant to be, 'a fellowship of creative heaven-led souls' with power to fulfil its vocation of transforming the world.

'Letter to the Prayer Group, Lent 1941,' *The Fruits of the Spirit*

First Sunday in Lent

GOD AND SELF-LOVE

FOR God, not man, is the first term of religion: and our first step in religion is the acknowledgement that He Is. All else is the unfolding of those truths about His life and our life, which this fact of facts involves. I believe in One God. We begin there; not with our own needs, desires, feelings, or obligations. Were all these abolished, His independent splendour would remain, as the Truth which gives its meaning to the world. So we begin by stating with humble delight our belief and trust in the most concrete, most rich of all realities—God. Yet even the power to do this reflects back again to Him, and witnesses to His self-giving to the soul. For Christianity is not a pious reverie, a moral system or a fantasy life; it is a revelation, adapted to our capacity, of the Realities which control life. Those Realities must largely remain unknown to us; limited little creatures that we are. God, as Brother Giles said, is a great mountain of corn from which man, like a sparrow, takes a grain of wheat: yet even that grain of wheat, which is as much as we can carry away, contains all the essentials of our life. We are to carry it carefully and eat it gratefully: remembering with awe the majesty of the mountain from which it comes.

The first thing this vast sense of God does for us, is to deliver us from the imbecilities of religious self-love and self-assurance; and sink our little souls in the great life of the race, in and upon which this One God in His mysterious independence is always working, whether we notice it or not. When that sense of His unique reality gets dim and stodgy, we must go back and begin there once more; saying with the Psalmist, 'All my fresh springs are in thee.' Man, said Christ, is nourished by every word that proceeds out of the mouth of God. Not the words we expect, or persuade ourselves that we have heard; but those unexpected words He really utters, sometimes by the mouths of the most unsuitable people, sometimes through apparently unspiritual events, sometimes secretly within the soul. Therefore seeking God, and listening to God, is an important part of the business of human life: and this is the essence of prayer. We do something immense, almost unbelievable, when we enter that world of prayer, for then we deliberately move out towards that transcendent Being whom Christianity declares to be the one Reality: a Reality revealed to us in three ways as a Creative Love, a Rescuing Love, and an Indwelling, all-pervading Love, and in each of those three ways claiming and responding to our absolute trust. Prayer is the give-and-take between the little souls of men and that three-fold Reality.

The School of Charity

Monday of the First Week in Lent

GOD MAKES, LOVES, KEEPS

IF the Reality of God were small enough to be grasped, it would not be great enough to be adored; and so our holiest privilege would go. 'I count not myself to have grasped; but as one that has been grasped, I press on,' says Saint Paul. But if all real knowledge here is a humbly delighted knowledge of our own ignorance—if, as the dying artist said, 'The word we shall use most when we get to heaven will be "Oh!"'—still we can realize something of what it means, to consider our world from this point of view. It means that everything we are given to deal with—including ourselves and our psychological material, however intractable—is the result of the creative action of a personal Love, who despises nothing that He has made. We, then, cannot take the risk of despising anything; and any temptation to do so must be attributed to our ignorance, stupidity or self-love, and recognized as something which distorts our vision of Reality.

'He showed me a little thing,' says Julian of Norwich, 'the quantity of a hazel nut in the palm of my hand; and it was as round as a ball. I looked thereupon with the eye of my understanding and thought: *What may this be?* And it was answered generally thus: *It is all that is made.* . . . In this Little Thing I saw three properties. The first is that God made it, the second is that God loveth it, the third, that God keepeth it.'

That is a saint's comment on the first article of her Creed. It is a vision that takes much living-out in a world in which injustice and greed are everywhere manifest; full too of tendencies which we are able to recognize as evil, and of misery and failure which seem the direct result of corporate stupidity and self-love, offering us ceaseless opportunities for the expression of disapproval and disgust, and often tempting to despair. 'All-thing hath the Being by the Love of God,' says Julian again. And then we think of a natural order shot through with suffering, marred at every point by imperfection, maintained by mutual destruction; a natural order which includes large populations of vermin, and the flora and fauna of infectious disease. It is easy to be both sentimental and theological over the more charming and agreeable aspects of Nature. It is very difficult to see its essential holiness beneath disconcerting and hostile appearances with an equable and purified sight; with something of the large, disinterested Charity of God.

To stand alongside the generous Creative Love, maker of all things visible and invisible (including those we do not like) and see them with the eyes of the Artist-Lover is the secret of sanctity. St. Francis did this with a singular perfection; but we know the price that he paid. So too that rapt and patient lover of all life, Charles Darwin, with his great, self-forgetful interest in the humblest and tiniest forms of life—not because they were useful to him, but for their own sakes—fulfilled one part of our Christian duty far better than many Christians do. It is a part of the life of prayer, which is our small attempt to live the life of Charity, to consider the whole creation with a deep and selfless reverence; enter into its wonder, and find in it the mysterious intimations of the Father of Life, maker of all things, Creative Love.

The School of Charity

Tuesday of the First Week in Lent

CREATION, CHANGE, HOLINESS

BUT the creative action of the Spirit penetrates the whole of life, and is felt by us in all sorts of ways. If our idea of that creative action is so restricted that we fail to recognize it working within the homely necessities and opportunities of our visible life, we may well suspect the quality of those invisible experiences to which we like to give spiritual status. 'I found Him very easily among the pots and pans,' said Saint Teresa, 'The duties of my position take precedence of everything else,' said Elizabeth Leseur; pinned down by those duties to a life which was a constant check on the devotional practices she loved. She recognized the totality of God's creative action, penetrating and controlling the whole web of life.

A genuine inner life must make us more and more sensitive to that moulding power, working upon His creation at every level, not at one alone: and especially to the constant small but expert touches, felt in and through very homely events, upon those half-made, unsteady souls which are each the subject of His detailed care. A real artist will give as much time and trouble to a miniature two inches square, as to the fresco on the Cathedral wall. The true splendour and heart-searching beauty of the Divine Charity is not seen in those cosmic energies which dazzle and confound us; but in the transcendent power which stoops to an intimate and cherishing love, the grave and steadfast Divine action, sometimes painful and sometimes gentle, on the small unfinished soul. It is an unflickering belief in this, through times of suffering and conflict, apathy and desperation, in a life filled with prosaic duties and often empty of all sense of God, that the Creed demands of all who dare recite it. . . .

Jesus chose, as the most perfect image of that action, the working of yeast in dough. The leavening of meal must have seemed to ancient men a profound mystery, and yet something on which they could always depend. Just so does the supernatural enter our natural life, working in the hiddenness, forcing the new life into every corner and making the dough expand. If the dough were endowed with consciousness, it would not feel very comfortable while the yeast was working. Nor, as a rule, does our human nature feel very comfortable under the transforming action of God: steadily turning one kind of love into another kind of love, desire into charity, clutch into generosity, *Eros* into *Agape*. Creation is change, and, change is often painful and mysterious to us. Spiritual creation means a series of changes, which at last produce, Holiness, God's aim for men.

The School of Charity

Wednesday of the First Week in Lent

GOD AND SELF-OFFERING

'O SUPPORT me,' says Newman, 'as I proceed in this great, awful, happy change, with the grace of Thy unchangeableness. My unchangeableness, here below, is perseverance in changing.' The inner life consists in an enduring of this deep transforming process. The chief object of prayer is to help it on: not merely for our own soul's sake, but for a reason which lifts the devotional life above all pettiness—because this is part of the great creative action which is lifting up humanity to the supernatural order, turning the flour and water of our common nature into the living Bread of Eternal Life. So, the first movement of our prayer must surely be a self-giving to this total purpose, whatever discipline and suffering it may involve for us. . . .

Our entire confidence in that One God who is the Creator of all things, the Father of all His creation, and whose wisdom 'sweetly orders' the working out of His undeclared design, must include such mysterious operations of grace as this. Again and again the sufferings of His children are made part of the yeast by which He changes and sanctifies all life. In our own inward life and prayer, this must mean a perpetual and peaceful self-offering for the hidden purposes of the Divine Charity, whatever they may be; and especially the sacred privilege of giving a creative quality to all pain. This is perhaps what von Hügel had in mind, when he spoke of 'getting our suffering well mixed up with our prayer. . . .'

The same principle applies to our own daily existence. 'The Kingdom of Heaven,' the supernatural order, is like yeast. And we are required to be part of the Kingdom of Heaven: sons and daughters of God. That means that we too have our share in the creative process. We live and die within the workshop; used as tools if we are merely dull and uninterested, but accepted as pupils and partners with our first movement of generosity in action, prayer or love. The implications of that truth must be worked out within each separate life: beginning where we are, content if our handful of meal can make a cottage loaf, not indulging spiritual vanity with large vague dreams about ovens full of beautiful brioches. Most of us when we were children managed sometimes to get into the kitchen; a wonderful experience with the right kind of cook. A whole world separated the cook who let us watch her make the cake, from the cook who let us make a little cake of our own. Then we were filled with solemn interest, completely satisfied, because we were anticipating the peculiar privilege of human beings; making something real, sharing the creative work of God. We, in our measure, are allowed to stand beside Him; making little things, contributing our action to His great action on life. So we must use the material of life faithfully, with a great sense of responsibility; and especially our energy of prayer, with a due remembrance of its awful power.

The School of Charity

Thursday of the First Week in Lent

GOD AND PRAYER

'IN faith,' says Kierkegaard, 'the self bases itself transparently on the power which created it.' The whole life of prayer is indeed a committal of our separate lives into God's hand, a perpetual replacing of the objective attitude by the personal and abandoned attitude; and though a certain tension, suffering and bewilderment are inevitable to our situation, yet there is with this a deep security. The pawn does not know what will be required of it or what may be before it; but its relation with the Player is always direct and stable, and the object of the Player is always the good of the pawn. 'Our souls are God's delight, not because of anything they do for Him, but because of what He does for them. All He asks of them is to accept with joy His indulgence, His generosity, His Fatherly love. Consider all your devotion to God in this way, and do not worry any more about what you are or are not. Be content to be the object of His mercy and look at nothing else. . . .'

Christ seems to have been deeply aware of the fragility of human nature; the folly of heroics, the danger of demanding or attempting too much. Watch and pray, that ye enter not into temptation. The spirit may be willing; but do not forget your lowly origin, the flesh is weak. Therefore, even in your abandonment, remain spiritually alert. Watch steadily. Gaze at God: keep your minds attuned to His reality and His call, and so elude the distractions that surround you. Pray. Seek His face. Lift up to Him your heart and speak to Him as one friend to another. Reach out towards Him in confident love. 'By two wings,' says Thomas a Kempis, 'is man borne up from earthly things, that is to say with plainness and cleanness: plainness is in the intent and cleanness is in the love. The good, true, and plain intent looketh toward God, but the clean love maketh assay and tasteth His sweetness.' So doing, you are drawn more and more deeply into His life, and have less and less to fear from competing attractions, longings and demands.

Abba

Friday of the First Week in Lent

GOD AND COMMITMENT

'UNTO Him who is everywhere,' says Saint Augustine, 'we come by love and not by navigation.' Talk of the 'Mystic Way' and its stages, or the 'degrees of Love,' may easily deceive us unless the Divine immanence, priority, and freedom be ever kept in mind. We may think of the soul's essential being as ever lying within the thought of God; and, equally, of His creative love as dwelling and acting within that soul's ground. These are contrasting glimpses of that total Truth 'of which no man may think.' And the true life of the spirit requires such a gradual self-abandonment to that prevenient and all-penetrating Presence that we become at last its unresisting agents; are formed and shaped under its gradual pressure, and can receive from moment to moment the needed impulsions and lights. . . .

Here we find a place for that mysterious attraction or compulsion which is perhaps the most striking of the ordinary evidences of the Holy Spirit's action on souls. The persistent inexplicable pressure towards one course—the curious attraction to one special kind of devotion or of service—the blocking of the obvious path, and the opening of another undesired path—all these witness to the compelling and moulding power of the living Spirit; taking, and if we respond, receiving the gift of our liberty and our will.

This indeed is what the spiritual life has always seemed to the greatest, humblest, and most enlightened souls; whatever symbols they may use in their efforts to communicate it. It is God, vividly and intimately present in all things and in us, ever setting the demand of His achieved Perfection over against the seething energies of His creative love, Who works in and through that world of things on us. And He demands our entire subjection to His creative action, our endurance of His secret chemistry; that He may work through and in us on the world.

The Golden Sequence

Saturday of the First Week in Lent

GOD AND HIS SAINTS

THE inner life means an ever-deepening awareness of all this: the slowly growing and concrete realization of a Life and a Spirit within us immeasurably exceeding our own, and absorbing, transmuting, supernaturalizing our lives by all ways and at all times. It means the loving sense of God, as so immeasurably beyond us as to keep us in a constant attitude of humblest awe— and yet so deeply and closely with us, as to invite our clinging trust and loyal love. This, it seems to me, is what theological terms like Transcendence and Immanence can come to mean to us when re-interpreted in the life of prayer. . . . A saint is simply a human being whose soul has thus grown up to its full stature, by full and generous response to its environment, God. He has achieved a deeper, bigger life than the rest of us, a more wonderful contact with the mysteries of the Universe; a life of infinite possibility, the term of which he never feels that he has reached. . . .

The saintly and simple Curé d'Ars was once asked the secret of his abnormal success in converting souls. He replied that it was done by being very indulgent to others and very hard on himself; a recipe which retains all its virtue still. And this power of being outwardly genial and inwardly austere, which is the real Christian temper, depends entirely on the use we make of the time set apart for personal religion. It is always achieved if courageously and faithfully sought; and there are no heights of love and holiness to which it cannot lead, no limits to the power which it can exercise over the souls of men.

We have the saints to show us that these things are actually possible: that one human soul can rescue and transfigure another, and can endure for it redemptive hardship and pain. We may allow that the saints are specialists; but they are specialists in a career to which all Christians are called. They have achieved, as it were, the classic status. They are the advance guard of the army; but we, after all, are marching in the main ranks. The whole army is dedicated to the same supernaturai cause; and we ought to envisage it as a whole, and to remember that every one of us wears the same uniform as the saints, has access to the same privileges, is taught the same drill and fed with the same food. The difference between them and us is a difference in degree, not in kind. They possess, and we most conspicuously lack, a certain maturity and depth of soul; caused by the perfect flowering in them of self-oblivious love, joy and peace.

Concerning the Inner Life

Second Sunday in Lent

THE INCARNATION

IT is plain that such a religion as Christianity, which has for its object the worship of the Divine self-revealed in history, the Logos incarnate in time and space—which seeks and finds God self-given, in and through the littleness of the manger, and the shamefulness of the Cross—is closely bound up with a sacramental interpretation of life. Christ, as Bérulle said so deeply and so boldly, is 'Himself the major sacrament'; the visible sign of the nature of the Eternal God, and the medium of that Eternal God's self-giving to men. And the Church, as His Mystical Body, the organ of His continued presence, lives with a sacramental life from which the reality and power of the specific Christian sacraments proceed, and which indeed gives to them their credentials. This precision, this apparent canalizing of a grace and power which are felt by the religious soul to be boundless in generosity and unconditioned in action, and operative throughout the whole of life, repels many spiritual minds. They can easily accept a diffused sacramentalism; but reject the notion of a special and ordained channel of grace. Nevertheless the distinctness of the Holy will never be sufficiently realized by us, unless His self-giving be apprehended as coming to man the creature in a special sense by particular paths; held sacred, and kept for Himself alone. And this means sacraments. The deep conviction of the Platonist that everything is a shadow and out-ward sign of a deeper and more enduring reality, is indeed precious as far as it goes; and is justified in those rare moments when the lovely veil is lifted and we catch a glimpse of greater loveliness behind. But this can never be enough for Christianity; which discloses a real God to real men by means of a real life and death in space and time. And here the law of belief must be the law of worship too. *Worship*

Monday of the Second Week in Lent

GOD AND THE TEMPORAL

St. John of the Cross, at the end of one of his great mystical poems, exclaims suddenly, 'How delicately Thou teachest love to me'! Perhaps if we realized more fully all that is implied in this utterance of one of the greatest of the contemplative saints, so wide and deep in his experience of the realities of the spiritual world, we should not be quite so hurried and full of assurance in constructing our clumsy diagrams of the delicate and subtle processes of God; so rigid in our exclusions, so horribly crude in our conceptions and demands. Perhaps this saying might even give us the beginning of a vision of God, as a Presence of unchanging Love and Beauty; teaching the race through history, and each soul through and within those faculties which have been evolved from our animal past. It might persuade us that a supercilious contempt of history and the time-process, an effort to achieve the Eternal by the mere rejection of the temporal, is hostile to the truest and richest theism. Such a lofty refusal of the common experience, such an attempt to get out of our own skins and elude the discipline of our humbling limitations, merely defeats its own end. Rather the faithful acceptance of history, a genial sharing in the experience of the race, is required of an incarnational religion: a full use of, and entrance into, that general scene within which the Eternal penetrates time, and the little creature of time can ascend to consciousness of the Eternal. Thus the right attitude of religion towards history is that of complete and humble acceptance, not rejection. Indeed, all the grestest supernatural experiences of men are found when we investigate them, to require and arise within a rich historical environment.

Man and the Supernatural

Tuesday of the Second Week in Lent

THE DIVINE CONDESCENSION

In its poetic elaborations of history—and these began almost at once—Christian genius has not failed to emphasize the paradox of the Unlimited thus revealed within humblest limitations. . . .

A carpenter's baby. Thirty years of obscure village life. A young man, of whose secret growth nothing is revealed to us, coming with a crowd to be baptized by a religious revivalist. A refusal of all self-regarding or spectacular use of that immense spiritual power and effortless authority which the records so plainly reveal. Unlimited compassion especially extended to the most sinful, blundering, sickly, and unattractive among men. A self-oblivion so perfect that we do not even notice it. A balanced life of fellowship and lonely prayer. A genial love of, and yet a perfect detachment from, all human and natural things. Unflinching acceptance of a path that pointed to suffering, humiliation, failure and death. At last, a condemned fanatic agonizing between two thieves. These were the chief external incidents which marked the full expression of the Supernatural in terms of human personality. Yet within this sequence of transitory acts all sensitive spirits felt and still feel the external *state*, the interior life of Christ hidden in God, of which these 'mysteries' are the sacramental expressions in space and time. Each scene in its own manner makes a sudden rift, and discloses a new tract of the supernatural world; and this with an even greater and more humbling splendour, with each advance of the seeing soul.

And indeed it is above all when we see a human spirit, knowing its own power, choose the path of sacrifice instead of the path of ambition: when we see human courage and generosity blazing out on the heroic levels in the shadow of death; the human agony and utter self-surrender of Gethsemane, the accepted desolation of the Cross, that we recognize a love and holiness which point beyond the world. There we discern that mysterious identity of Revealer and Revealed, that complete appropriation of personality to the manifestation of God, which it is the special province of the Fourth Evangelist to emphasize.

Man and the Supernatural

Wednesday of the Second Week in Lent

THE HOLINESS OF THINGS

THE Incarnation means that the Eternal God enters our common human life with all the energy of His creative love, to transform it, to exhibit to us its richness, its unguessed significance; speaking our language, and showing us His secret beauty on our own scale.

Thus the spiritual life does not begin in an arrogant attempt at some peculiar kind of other-worldliness, a rejection of ordinary experience. It begins in the humble recognition that human things can be very holy, full of God; whereas high-minded speculations about His nature need not be holy at all. Since all life is engulfed in Him, He can reach out to us anywhere and at any level. The depth and richness of His Eternal Being are unknown to us. Yet Christianity declares that this unsearchable Life, which is in essence a self-giving Love, and is wholly present wherever it loves, so loved this world as to desire to reveal within it the deepest secret of His thought; appearing within and through His small, fugitive, imperfect creatures, in closest union with humanity. In the beginning was the Word: and the Word was God, and without Him was not anything made that hath been made: and the Word became flesh and dwelt among us.

That seems immense. A complete philosophy is contained in it. And then we come down to the actual settlement of this supreme event, and at once all our notions of the suitable and the significant are set aside; and moreover, all our pet values reversed. A Baby, just that; a Baby, born in the most unfortunate circumstances. The extremes of the transcendent and the homely are suddenly brought together in the disconcerting revelation of reality. The hard life of the poor, its ceaseless preoccupation with the lowliest of human needs and duties, the absolute surrender and helplessness, the half-animal status of babyhood; all this is the chosen vehicle for the unmeasured inpouring of the Divine Life and Love. So too the strange simplicity of its beginning both rebukes and reassures us. It is like a quiet voice speaking in our deepest prayer: 'The Lord is with thee . . .' and calling forth the one and only answer, 'Behold the handmaid of the Lord, be it unto me according to thy Word'! Humble self-abandonment is found and declared to be enough to give us God. First in one way and then in another, all the incidents which cluster round the mystery of the Incarnation seem designed to show us this; the simplest yet the deepest truth about His relation to the soul.

The School of Charity

Thursday of the Second Week in Lent

THE INTERIOR LIFE

WHEN Saint Paul described our mysterious human nature as a 'Temple of the Holy Spirit'—a created dwelling-place or sanctuary of the uncreated and invisible Divine Life—he was stating in the strongest possible terms a view of our status, our relation to God, which has always been present in Christianity; and is indeed implicit in the Christian view of Reality. But that statement as it stands seems far too strong for most of us. We do not feel in the very least like the temples of Creative Love. We are more at ease with Saint Teresa, when she describes the soul as an 'interior castle'—a roomy mansion, with various floors and apartments from the basement upwards; not all devoted to exalted uses, not always in a satisfactory state. And when, in a more homely mood, she speaks of her own spiritual life as 'becoming solid like a house,' we at last get something we can grasp.

The soul's house, that interior dwelling-place which we all possess, for the upkeep of which we are responsible—a place in which we can meet God, or from which in a sense we can exclude God—that is not too big an idea for us. Though no imagery drawn from the life of sense can ever be adequate to the strange and delicate contacts, tensions, demands and benedictions of the life that lies beyond sense: though the important part of every parable is that which it fails to express: still, here is a conception which can be made to cover many of the truths that govern the interior life of prayer.

First, we are led to consider the position of the house. However interesting and important its peculiarities may seem to the tenant, it is not as a matter of fact an unusually picturesque and interesting mansion made to an original design, and set in its own grounds with no other building in sight. Christian spirituality knows nothing of this sort of individualism. It insists that we do not inhabit detached residences, but are parts of a vast spiritual organism; that even the most hidden life is never lived for itself alone. Our soul's house forms part of the vast City of God. Though it may not be an important mansion with a frontage on the main street, nevertheless it shares all the obligations and advantages belonging to the city as a whole. It gets its water from the main, and its light from the general supply. The way we maintain and use it must have reference to our civic responsibilities.

The House of the Soul

Friday of the Second Week in Lent

THE ROOT OF THE INTERIOR LIFE

IT is true that God creates souls in a marvellous liberty and variety. The ideals of the building-estate tell us nothing about the Kingdom of Heaven. It is true also, that the furnishing of our rooms and cultivation of our garden is largely left to our personal industry and good taste. Still, in a general way, we must fall in with the city's plan; and consider, when we hang some new and startling curtains, how they will look from the street. However intense the personal life of each soul may be, that personal life has got out of proportion, if it makes us forget our municipal obligations and advantages; for our true significance is more than personal, it is bound up with the fact of our status as members of a supernatural society. So into all the affairs of the little house there should enter a certain sense of the city, and beyond this of the infinite world in which the city stands: some awe-struck memory of our double situation, at once so homely and so mysterious. We must each maintain unimpaired our unique relation with God; yet without forgetting our intimate contact with the rest of the city, or the mesh of invisible life which binds all the inhabitants in one.

For it is on the unchanging Life of God, as on a rock, that the whole city is founded. That august and cherishing Spirit is the atmosphere which bathes it, and fills each room of every little house—quickening, feeding and sustaining. He is the one Reality which makes us real; and, equally, the other houses too. 'If I am not in Thee,' said St. Augustine, 'then I am not at all.' We are often urged to think of the spiritual life as a personal adventure, a ceaseless hustle forward; with all its

44

meaning condensed in the 'perfection' of the last stage. But though progress, or rather growth, is truly in it, such growth, in so far as it is real can only arise from, and be conditioned by, a far more fundamental relation—the growing soul's abidingness in God.

The House of the Soul

Saturday of the Second Week in Lent

TIME AND ETERNITY

NEXT, what type of house does the soul live in? It is a two-story house. The psychologist too often assumes that it is a one-roomed cottage with a mud floor; and never even attempts to go upstairs. The extreme transcendentalist sometimes talks as though it were perched in the air, like the lake dwellings of our primitive ancestors, and had no ground floor at all. A more humble attention to facts suggests that neither of these simplifications is true. We know that we have a ground floor, a natural life biologically conditioned, with animal instincts and affinities; and that this life is very important, for it is the product of the divine creativity—its builder and maker is God. But we know too that we have an upper floor, a supernatural life, with supernatural possibilities, a capacity for God; and that this, man's peculiar prerogative, is more important still. If we try to live on one floor alone we destroy the mysterious beauty of our human vocation; so utterly a part of the fugitive and creaturely life of this planet and yet so deeply coloured by Eternity; so entirely one with the world of nature, and yet, 'in the Spirit,' a habitation of God. 'Thou madest him lower than the angels, to crown him with glory and worship.' We are created both in Time and in Eternity, not truly one but truly two; and every thought, word and act must be subdued to the dignity of that double situation in which Almighty God has placed and companions the childish spirit of man.

Therefore a full and wholesome spiritual life can never consist in living upstairs, and forgetting to consider the ground floor and its homely uses and needs; thus ignoring the humbling fact that those upper rooms are entirely supported by it. Nor does it consist in the constant, exasperated investigation of the shortcomings of the basement. When Saint Teresa said that her prayer had become 'solid like a house,' she meant that its foundations now went down into the lowly but firm ground of human nature, the concrete actualities of the natural life: and on those solid foundations, its walls rose up towards heaven. The strength of the house consisted in that intimate welding together of the divine and the human, which she found in its perfection in the humanity of Christ. There, in the common stuff of human life which He blessed by His presence, the saints have ever seen the homely foundations of holiness. Since we are two-story creatures, called to a natural and a supernatural status, both sense and spirit must be rightly maintained, kept in order, consecrated to the purposes of the city, if our full obligations are to be fulfilled. The house is built for God; to reflect, on each level, something of His unlimited Perfection. Downstairs that general rightness of adjustment to all this-world obligations, which the ancients called the quality of Justice; and the homely virtues of Prudence, Temperance and Fortitude reminding us of our creatureliness, our limitations, and so humbling and disciplining us. Upstairs, the heavenly powers of Faith, Hope and Charity; tending towards the Eternal, nourishing our life towards God, and having no meaning apart from God.

The House of the Soul

Third Sunday in Lent

THE TWO LOVES

THERE is a wonderful chapter in Ruysbroeck's *Book of the Twelve Béguines* in which he describes the life of one who has achieved this state, as 'ministering to the world without in love and in mercy; whilst inwardly abiding in simplicity, in stillness, and in utter peace.' Reading it, we remember that it was said of Ruysbroeck himself, that supreme mystic, that during the years in which he was a parish priest in Brussels, he went to and fro in the streets of the city 'with his mind perpetually lifted up into God.' He was ministering to the world without in love and mercy; whilst inwardly abiding in simplicity, stillness, and utter peace. Action, effort and tension, then, are to be the outward expression and substance of such a life of spiritual creativeness; yet all this is to hang on and be nurtured by an inward abidingness in simplicity, stillness and peace. We are called upon to carry the Eternal and Unchanging right through every detail of our changeful active life, because and by means of our daily secret recourse to and concentration upon it. Is it not in practising this lovely and costly art, gradually getting at home with it, that we more and more transmute and deify the very substance even of our temporal life? thus more and more doing the special work of the human soul, as a link between the worlds of spirit and sense. . . .

In other words: Our deepest life consists in a willed correspondence with the world of Spirit, and this willed correspondence, which is prayer, is destined to fulfil itself along two main channels; in love towards God and in love towards humanity—two loves which at last and at their highest become one love. Sooner or later, in varying degrees, the power and redeeming energy of God will be manifested through those who thus reach

48

out in desire, first towards Him, and then towards other souls. And we, living and growing personalities, are required to become ever more and more spiritualized, ever more and more persuasive, more and more deeply real; in order that we may fulfil this Divine purpose.

Concerning the Inner Life

Monday of the Third Week in Lent

HOLINESS AND THE TWO LOVES

THIS is not mere pious fluff. This is a terribly practical job; the only way in which we can contribute to the bringing in of the Kingdom of God. Humanitarian politics will not do it. Theological restatement will not do it. Holiness *will* do it. And for this growth towards holiness, it seems that it is needful to practise, and practise together, both that genuine peaceful recollection in which the soul tastes, and really knows that the Lord is sweet, inwardly abiding in His stillness and peace; and also the suffering, effort and tension required of us unstable human creatures, if we are to maintain that interior state and use it for the good of other men. This ideal is so rich, that in its wholeness it has only been satisfied once. Yet it is so elastic, that within it every faithful personality can find a place and opportunity of development. It means the practice of both attachment and detachment; the most careful and loving fulfilment of all our varied this-world obligations, without any slackening of attachment to the other-worldly love.

And if we want a theoretical justification of such a scheme of life, surely we have it in the central Christian doctrine of the Incarnation? For does not this mean the Eternal, Changeless God reaching out to win and eternalize His creatures by contact through personality? that the direct action of Divine Love on man is through man; and that God requires our growth in personality, in full being, in order that through us His love and holiness can more and more fully be expressed? And our Lord's life in ministry supported by much lonely prayer gives us the classic pattern of human correspondence with this, our two-fold environment. The saints tried to imitate that pattern more and more closely; and as they did so, their personality expanded and shone with love and power. They show us in history a growth and transformation of character which we are not able to grasp; yet which surely ought to be the Christian norm? In many cases they were such ordinary, even unpromising people when they began; for the real saint is neither a special creature nor a spiritual freak. He is just a human being in whom has been fulfilled the great aspiration of St. Augustine— 'My life shall be a real life, being wholly full of Thee.' And as that real life, that interior union with God grows, so too does the saints' self-identification with humanity grow. They do not stand aside wrapped in delightful prayers and feeling pure and agreeable to God. They go right down into the mess; and there right down in the mess, they are able to radiate God because they possess Him.

Concerning the Inner Life

Tuesday of the Third Week in Lent

A LETTER TO A FRIEND: PRIDE

To the alarming list of innate vices which you have managed to get together I should like to add another: Pride. All this preoccupation with your own imperfection is not humility, but an insidious form of spiritual pride. What do you *expect* to be? A saint? There are desperately few of them: and even they found their faults, which are the raw material of sanctity remember, take a desperate lot of working up. You know best when and how you fall into these various pitfalls. Try and control yourself when you see the temptation coming. (*Sometimes* you will succeed, which is so much to the good.) Pull yourself up and make an act of contrition when you catch yourself doing any of the things. *Never* allow yourself to be pessimistic about your own state. Look outwards instead of inwards: and when you are inclined to be depressed and think you are getting on badly, make an act of thanksgiving instead, because others are getting on well. The object of your salvation is God's Glory, not your happiness. Remember it is all one to the angels whether you or another give Him the holiness He demands.

So, be content to help on His kingdom, remaining yourself in the lowest place. Merge yourself in the great life of the Christian family. Make intercessions, work for it, keep it in your mind. You have tied yourself up so tight in that accursed individualism of yours—the source of *all* your difficulties— that it is a marvel you can breathe at all.

I hope you are going to get hold of a little personal work amongst the poor when you can? As for the inclination to cut connection with other people, THAT must be fought tooth and nail, please. Go out as much as you can, and enter into the interests of others, however twaddley. They are all part of life, remember; and life, for you, is *divine*.

As to the last crime on your list, however, 'dislike of pain,' you need not take a very desponding view. My dear child, *everyone* dislikes pain, really—except a few victims of religious and other forms of hysteria. Even the martyrs, it has been said, had 'less joy of their triumph because of the pain they endured.' They did not *want* the lions: but they knew how to 'endure the Cross' when it came. Do not worry your head about such things as this: but trust God and live your life bit by bit as it comes.

There. God bless you.

The Letters of Evelyn Underhill

Letter dated St. Patrick's Day, 1909

Wednesday of the Third Week in Lent

ANOTHER LETTER: THE CROSS

I DO not think you have ever made the Cross the centre of your life *really*. I do not quite know what you have made the centre, but it looks as though it cannot be that. And you have got to, you know. Nothing else will do. And if you do not accept it deliberately, why then it will be forced on you in some subtle and ingenious way, as it is at the present moment. And by struggling and tiring yourself out, you make it worse and add physical and mental fatigue to your spiritual troubles. *Accept* what you are having, quite simply and obediently. Take it as it comes. Do not 'will' or 'want' this or that; however virtuous and edifying your wishes may be. All such willings presuppose that you know better than the Spirit of God. And do not get into a despairing condition. These experiences are a perfectly normal part of the spiritual life: which is *not* designed on the lines of a 'Pleasant Sunday Afternoon.'

As to what you ought to do, it is very difficult to advise anyone else in this sort of condition. But I feel pretty sure you ought not to shirk church and your ordinary times of prayer. Only, do not on any account struggle AT ALL to feel things or get into communion or anything like that. Surrender yourself altogether and be quite quiet. The thing is not in your hands at the present. You are just to remain true to your colours. Leave off mental prayer and meditation. Stick to formal prayer. And it would be well to leave those you ordinarily use, and take for the time to quite fresh ones. I do not know how long you spend in prayer, but very likely now you will NOT be able to spend so long. There is no object in exhausting yourself. You have been long poring over the whole thing too much; instead of letting it happen, like a spell of bad weather.

I would rather you did some external good works, and thought less for the present about your soul. (I do not mean by this that I think grate-cleaning a proper substitute for church.) I wonder whether you have let your physical health run down and got nervous: because of course that accounts for a lot, and must not be confused with the other.

This sounds an odiously unsympathetic letter, and sort of easy and superior. But it is not meant to be really.

I know quite well what these states are like, and how dreary it is; and do not behave at all well under them. But I know too that surrender is the ONLY way out of them. Humility and WILL-ING suffering have got to be learned if we want to be Christians, and some people learn them by boredom instead of by torture. But once you really surrender it is extraordinary how the nastiness goes and you perceive that it *was* the 'shade of His Hand out-stretched caressingly.'

The Letters of Evelyn Underhill

Letter dated February 7, 1911

Thursday of the Third Week in Lent

SEVEN ROADS TO HELL

THERE are seven dispositions in us which specially block the action of God and are hostile to the Holy; which twists our souls out of shape. Theology calls them the seven deadly sins—deadly because once they get their claws into us they tend to spiritual extinction instead of spiritual life.

1. Pride, uppishness, the great instinct of self-regard. No one can see straight in religion till they get rid of that.
2. Envy—an inimical, snarky attitude to others, ill-wind in all, even its most subtle and refined forms.
3. Anger, the combative instinct, turbulence, emotional uproar, self-centred vehemence, the negation of Peace.
4. Sloth, the opposite number of wholesome zest, the deadly spirit of slackness, fed-up-ness, 'is it worth while-ness.'
5. Avarice, the possessive spirit, grab and hold-tight in all its manifestations.
6. Gluttony, intemperate enjoyment for its own sake of what is in reason good and allowable.
7. Lust—letting our instinct and emotional nature get the upper hand and leading us, instead of our leading it, being ruled by our longings.

Now we may feel prepared to repudiate some of these on sight, as having nothing to do with ordinary civilized life. We consider that we are not envious, avaricious, wrathful, greedy. It's not done! But it is not only our natural life that is concerned. Those tendencies are ingrained in human nature and infect the most subtle reaches of our personal and spiritual life too: they colour our prayer because genuine prayer reflects character.

For they all mean at bottom three great disorders of our power of love—loving wrong things, loving too much, loving too little.

Pride and avarice mean the drive of energy set towards our selves and our possessions. Lust and gluttony love too much. Sloth and envy love too little. They all turn up in our relation to the things God gives us to deal with—family, friends, work and the practice of religion. As we wake up more towards spiritual reality and our world grows, the form of our sinfulness probably changes. The great wrong instincts of self-importance, pugnacity, grab, self-indulgence, slackness, are still there, but gradually pass from cruder to more and more subtle forms— spiritual pride, spiritual envy, spiritual greed: these still lie in wait for souls who *believe* they want nothing but God.

The Mount of Purification

Friday of the Third Week in Lent

THE WAY

CHRISTIANITY, of course, has often been described as a 'life.' The early Christians themselves called it not a belief, but a 'way'— a significant fact, which the Church too quickly forgot; and the realist who wrote the Fourth Gospel called its founder both *the* life and *the* way. But these terms have been employed by all later theologians with discreet vagueness, have been accepted in the artistic rather than the scientific sense; with the result that Christianity as a life has meant almost anything, from obedience to a moral or even an ecclesiastical code at one end of the scale, to the enjoyment of peculiar spiritual sensations at the other. . . .

But where many of the greatest mystics have shown natural dread of the trials confronting them—inclined to cry with Suso, 'Oh, Lord, Thy tournaments last a very long time!'—Jesus seems to run almost eagerly to His fate. The surrender for which they fought, sometimes through years of anguish, is already His. The instinct for self-donation rules Him: it needs but opportunity for expression. Once the necessary course of life is clear to Him, He goes deliberately to the encounter of danger and persecution. With an ever clearer premonition of the result, He abandoned the wandering missionary life amongst the country towns of Galilee, and set His face towards Jerusalem: plainly warning His disciples that those who followed now did so at their personal risk; and adopted a course which must separate them from family and friends. They were come to the parting of the ways. Life was going forward to new and difficult levels, and those who would go with it must go in full consciousness of danger, inviting not shirking the opposition of the sensual world. This is the idea which is paraphrased by the Synoptics as the 'bearing of one's own cross'; a metaphor which has become charged for us with a deeply pathetic significance, but was in its origin exactly equivalent to the homely English proverb about 'putting the rope round one's own neck'—a plain invitation to loyalty and courage.

The Mystic Way

Saturday of the Third Week in Lent

DISTRACTION AND DRYNESS

It is one of the most distressing aspects of personal religion that we all waste so much of the very limited time which we are able to give it. The waste can be classified under two main heads: distraction and dryness. No one escapes these, but it concerns us all to reduce them as much as we can. Of dryness I will speak later. As to distraction, this is of two kinds, which we might call fundamental and mechanical. Fundamental distraction is really lack of attention; and lack of attention is really lack of interest. We are seldom distracted where we are truly keen—where the treasure is, the heart is sure to be. Saint Teresa's advice to her nuns, to 'get themselves some company when first they go to prayer' is one prescription for the cure of fundamental distractedness. Another, particularly suitable for those who find it impossible to forget the pressure of external cares and legitimate interests, consists in making those very cares and interests the subject-matter of the prayer, thus conquering the distraction by absorption instead of by conflict. Mechanical distraction, on the other hand, seems to be connected with the element of reverie which is present in meditation and mental prayer; and the difficulty, inherent in this type of thinking, of maintaining complete concentration. In such mechanical distraction the deeper soul remains steadfast in prayer, the will and intention do not vary; but recollection is disturbed by involuntary thoughts and images which perpetually pass across the field of consciousness. The remedy for this is a steady, patient training of the mind; the gradual formation of channels along which our devotional energies can flow. . . .

Finally, I want to say something about a factor which is always present in every developed life of prayer: the liability to spiritual dryness and blankness, painful to all fervent Christians, but specially distressing to those whose business it is to work in souls. The times when all your interest and sense of reality evaporate; when the language of religion becomes meaningless and you are quite unable, in any real sense, to pray. Everyone is so off-colour from time to time; and it is one of the great problems of the priest and religious teacher, to know how, under these conditions, he can best serve God and other souls. Now first of all, it is possible to reduce the intensity of such desolations—to use the technical term—by wise handling of yourselves; and here prudent self-treatment is plainly your duty—the dictates of grace and common sense coincide. The condition is largely psychological. It is a fatigue state; a reaction sometimes from excessive devotional fervour, sometimes from exacting spiritual work, which has exhausted the inner reserves of the soul. It almost always follows on any period of marked spiritual progress or enlightenment. In either case, the first point is, accept the situation quietly. Don't aggravate it, don't worry, don't dwell on it, don't have contrition about it; but turn, so far as you can, to some secular interest or recreation and '*wait* till the clouds roll by.' Many a priest ends every Sunday in a state of exhaustion in which he cannot possibly say his own prayers; in which, as one of them observed, the only gift of the Spirit in which he is able to take any interest is a hot bath. That is a toll levied by his psycho-physical limitations. Effort and resistance will only make it worse.

Concerning the Inner Life

Fourth Sunday in Lent

WORSHIP AND RESPONSE

WORSHIP, in all its grades and kinds, is the response of the creature to the Eternal: nor need we limit this definition to the human sphere. There is a sense in which we *may think* of the whole life of the Universe, seen and unseen, conscious and unconscious, as an act of worship, glorifying its Origin, Sustainer, and End. Only in some such context, indeed, can we begin to understand the emergence and growth of the spirit of worship in men, or the influence which it exerts upon their concrete activities. Thus worship may be overt or direct, unconscious or conscious. Where conscious, its emotional colour can range from fear through reverence to self-oblivious love. But whatever its form of expression may be, it is always a subject-object relationship; and its general existence therefore constitutes a damaging criticism of all merely subjective and immanental explanations of Reality. For worship is an acknowledgement of Transcendence; that is to say, of a Reality independent of the worshipper, which is always more or less deeply coloured by mystery, and which is there first. . . .

So, directly we take this strange thing Worship seriously, and give it the status it deserves among the various responses of men to their environment, we find that it obliges us to take up a particular attitude towards that environment. Even in its crudest form, the law of prayer—indeed the fact of prayer—is already the law of belief; since humanity's universal instinct to worship cannot be accounted for, if naturalism tells the whole truth about life. That instinct means the latent recognition of a metaphysical reality, standing over against physical reality, which men are driven to adore, and long to apprehend. In other words it is the implicit, even though unrecognized Vision of God—that disclosure of the Supernatural which is overwhelming, self-giving, and attractive all at once—which is the first cause of worship, from the puzzled upward glance of the primitive to the delighted self-oblation of the saint. Here, the human derived spirit perceives and moves towards its Origin and goal; even though that perception shares the imperfections and uncertainties of the temporal order, and is often embodied in crude and mistaken forms. Here man responds to the impact of Eternity, and in so doing learns the existence of Eternity; accepting his tiny place in that secret life of Creation, which consists in the praise, adoration, and manifestation of God. That is to say, he achieves his destiny.

Worship

Monday of the Fourth Week in Lent

WORSHIP AND REVELATION

Genuine Christian worship, whatever its special emphasis may be, always requires as its foundation belief in the one Holy and Eternal God, the Being of Beings, the 'Maker, Lover, and Keeper' of all life; utterly transcendent to His creation, and yet fully present with and in it, besetting, sustaining, moulding—above all loving—all that is made. Its object is a Reality 'higher than our highest yet more inward than our most inward part,' uniting within His mysterious Nature the cosmic and the personal, the extremes of tenderness and power. This majestic vision it shares to some extent with other great theistic religions—e.g. Judaism and Islam—and here the devotional expressions of many of its greatest masters of theocentric worship, such as St. Augustine, do not go beyond the language of the Hebrew Psalter, the Neoplatonic mystics, and the Sufi saints. But the peculiar note of Christianity is struck when, within this awed yet delighted recognition of the Eternal Godhead, we place as the focus of devotion one single revelation in time and space of His essential character—'the effulgence of his glory and the very image of his substance'—made in the person of Jesus Christ; and complete this by acknowledging the presence and power of His holy personal and eternal Spirit—His absolute Will and Love—at work within the world of Time. For this means that we discover and adore the Supernatural, in its independence and completeness, truly immanent in the natural; proceeding from the deeps of Absolute Being, yet charged with the self-giving ardour of Absolute Love.

Christian worship in its wholeness must include or imply such equal, loving, and costly responses to this threefold Reality as we find for example in the writings of St. Paul: awestruck adoration of the self-existent Eternal, 'the only Wise God,' total self-offering to Him in Christ, and an active and grateful recognition of the Holy Spirit of God, in His creative guiding and purifying action upon the Church and the soul. It involves, then, an adoring acknowledgement first of God's cosmic splendour and otherness, next to His redemptive and transfiguring action revealed in history, and last of His immanent guidance of life. The full Eucharistic canon . . . passing from the *Sanctus* to the commemoration of Christ's life and passion, and thence to an invocation of the Spirit, gives liturgical expression to this, the norm of Christian worship; and it is this constant association of the Eternal and temporal, the transcendent and incarnate, majesty and generous love, which gives that worship its unique character.

Worship

Tuesday of the Fourth Week in Lent

WORSHIP AND CHRIST

Since the Christian revelation is in its very nature historical—God coming the whole way to man, and discovered and adored within the arena of man's life at one point in time, in and through the Humanity of Christ—it follows that all the historical events and conditions of Christ's life form part of the vehicle of revelation. Each of them mediates God, disclosing some divine truth or aspect of divine love to us. Here lies the importance of the Christian year, with its recurrent memorials of the Birth, the Manhood, the Death and the Triumph of Jesus, as the framework of the Church's ordered devotion. By and in this ancient sequence, with its three great moments of Epiphany, Easter and Pentecost, its detailed demonstration in human terms of the mysteries of Incarnation and Redemption, the Christian soul is led out through succession to a contemplation of the eternal action of God. In Christ, and therefore in all the states and acts of Christ, history and eternity meet. Here, in One 'who lived and died and is alive evermore' the worshipper adores the abiding God, self-revealed among men. 'His resplendent figure lights up the whole liturgy.' Moreover, since in Christ the Christian sees God acting, each phase of His life is to be regarded as a theophany, and has a sacred significance. It is the expression of an interior state directly produced by God, a necessary part of the redemption action of God, and so invites a particular acknowledgement in worship. . . .

So, in that devout commemoration of the successive Mysteries of the life of Jesus, from Christmas to Easter and to their consummation in Pentecost, on which the liturgical year of the

66

Church is based, all the phases of human experience are lit up by the radiance of eternity and brought into relation with the inexhaustible revelation of God in the flesh: giving the Christian a model he can never equal but a standard to which he must ever seek to conform. The helplessness and humility of infancy, the long hidden period of discipline and growth, the lonely crisis and choice of the Temptation, above all the heart-shaking events of Holy Week, Easter and the Forty Days—all these become disclosures of the Supernatural made through and in man, and therefore having a direct application of man's need and experience. Each shows the Divine self-giving from a different angle; and so asks from man a humble gratitude and a generous response.

Worship

Wednesday of the Fourth Week in Lent

WORSHIP AND THE SAINTS

... Christian worship is never a solitary undertaking. Both on its visible and invisible sides, it has a thoroughly social and organic character. The worshipper, however lonely in appearance, comes before God as a member of a great family; part of the Communion of Saints, living and dead. His own small effort of adoration is offered 'in and for all.' The first words of the Lord's Prayer are always there to remind him of his corporate status and responsibility, in its double aspect. On one hand, he shares the great life and action of the Church, the Divine Society; however he may define this difficult term, or wherever he conceives its frontiers to be drawn. He is immersed in that life, nourished by its traditions, taught, humbled, and upheld by its saints. His personal life of worship, unable for long to maintain itself alone, has behind it two thousand years of spiritual culture, and around it the self-offerings of all devoted souls. Further, his public worship, and commonly his secret devotion too, are steeped in history and tradition; and apart from them, cannot be understood. There are few things more remarkable in Christian history than the continuity through many vicissitudes and under many disguises of the dominant strands in Christian worship. On the other hand the whole value of this personal life of worship abides in the completeness with which it is purified from all taint of egotism, and the selflessness and simplicity with which it is added to the common store. Here the individual must lose his life to find it; the longing for personal expression, personal experience, safety, joy, must more and more be swallowed up in Charity. For the goal alike of Christian sanctification and Christian worship is the ceaseless self-offering of the Church, in and with Christ her head, to the increase of the glory of God.

Worship

Thursday of the Fourth Week in Lent

GOD AND UNDERSTANDING

'THE utmost that we know of God,' says St. Thomas, 'is nothing in respect of that which He is.'

Such an outlook on the Unchanging redeems our prayer from pettiness, discounts our worries, brings a solemn selfless peace. Everything drops away except awe, longing, and humility. 'Whom have I in heaven but thee? and there is none upon earth that I desire beside thee.' The soul stands over against the eternal reality of the Universe, and finds there a friend and not a void. *Deus Meus!* My God! We have, in our creaturely weakness, a personal hold upon Infinite Reality. The Psalms are full of this exultant certitude. 'O God, thou art *my* God! early will I seek thee!' Saint Augustine is ever recurring to such thoughts: isolating, gazing at, the Fact of God. Thus to dwell upon the great keywords of religion gives depth and width to human prayer; clarifies the sight with which we look out upon the sky.

We turn to the window on the other side of Faith's tower. That looks out upon our homely, natural, changeful world. It shows us human life, conditions, problems, from the angle of faith; and the mystery of the Eternal self-revealed in human ways. That too is a wonderful and inspiring sight, enlightening the understanding. Though clouds pass over that landscape, storms come, seasons change, it is yet seen to be full of God's glory. The same unchanging light and life bathes the world we see out of each window. Jungle and city, church and market-place, the mostly homely and the most mysterious aspects of creation, are equally known as works of the Wisdom of God.

From this window the earth with its intricate life is perceived in the light of the Incarnation; God self-disclosed in and with us, as well as God over against us. The depth and mystery of Reality, its stern yet loving action, are revealed within the limitations of history, and in the here-and-now experience of men. We pierce the disconcerting veil of appearance, and discern that Holy Creativity, making, rectifying, and drawing all things to itself. At times a lovely glint transfigures even the smallest living things. We see the kitten play in Paradise. The humble inhabitants of the hedgerows suddenly reveal their origin, their kinship with God. At other times a deeper secret, the little golden rill of Holiness welling up from beyond the world of visible life, is glimpsed by us in the most unexpected situations. Yet there is no pink glass in this window. It blurs none of the dread facts; the ever-present evil, the baffling pain, the conflict and apparent failure and inequality of life. But from the angle of Faith these are seen in proportion, as material for the self-imparting of God; and for man's self-giving to God truly tabernacled among us. Through the clatter of the world, Faith hears an insistent call to purity and sweetness; and discerns in the tangle of life the perpetual emergence of an other-worldly beauty, which has its source and end in Him alone.

The House of the Soul

Friday of the Fourth Week in Lent

GOD, ACKNOWLEDGED OR NOT

Six hundred years ago Saint Francis, praying alone when he thought himself unobserved, found nothing to say but this: 'My God and All! What art Thou? And what am I?' And in spite of the modern knowledge we are so proud of, the human soul is saying that still.

As a matter of fact, those remarkable changes that strike us so much when we observe the modern scene are mostly on life's surface. There are very few changes at life's heart. That is why great literature, however ancient, always moves us and is always understood. It has to do with the unchanging heart of life. And it is in the heart, not on the surface, that the world of religion makes itself known. 'With Thee is the well of life, and in Thy light we see light.' Does the theory of relativity really make any difference to that? I do not think so. We do not, after all, reconstruct our married life every time we move into a new and larger flat. The old, sacred intimacies remain. So too, the move-out of the human mind into a new and larger physical world, which is, I suppose, the great fact of our time, does not make any real difference to the soul's relation to God; even though it may make some difference to the language in which we describe Him. And the reason in both cases is surely the same.

The reason is that the deepest and most sacred relationships between human creatures—man and wife, parent and child, teacher and disciple, friend and friend—and the yet deeper relationship between the human creature and its Keeper and Creator, God: these are real facts, which go on, and will go on, quite independently of what we think of them, or the degree in which we understand or feel them. If we treat these deep things with contempt, we merely cheapen our own lives. We do not make any difference to truth. If we leave them out, then we get a very incomplete picture of reality; the picture of a world which has an outside but no inside. But we do not alter reality. Clever as we are, we cannot manage that. Just as, if we choose to shut all our windows, the room certainly gets stuffy; but we do not alter the quality of the fresh air outside. So the reality of God, the living atmosphere of Spirit, maintains its unalterable pressure; whether we acknowledge it or not.

'The Inside of Life,' *Collected Papers*

Saturday of the Fourth Week in Lent

A FISH IN THE SEA

MYSTICS, trying to tell us of their condition, often say that they feel 'sunk in God like a fish in the sea.' We pass over these phrases very easily, and forget that they are the final result of a long struggle to find the best image for an admittedly imageless truth. Yet prayer is above all the act in which we give ourselves to our soul's true Patria; enter again that Ocean of God which is at once our origin and our inheritance, and there find ourselves mysteriously at home. And this strange, home-like feeling kills the dread which might overcome us, if we thought of the unmeasured depth beneath us, and the infinite extent and utter mystery of that Ocean into which we have plunged. As it is, a curious blend of confidence and entire abandonment keep us, because of our very littleness, in peace and joy: content with our limited powers and the limitless Love in which we are held. Nothing in all nature is so lovely and so vigorous, so perfectly at home in its environment, as a fish in the sea. Its surroundings give to it a beauty, quality, and power which is not its own. We take it out, and at once a poor, limp dull thing, fit for nothing, is gasping away its life. So the soul sunk in God, living the life of prayer, is supported, filled, transformed in beauty, by a vitality and a power which are not its own. The souls of the saints are so powerful because they are thus utterly immersed in the Spirit: their whole life is a prayer. The Life in which they live and move and have their being gives them something of its own quality. So long as they maintain themselves within it, they are adequate to its demands, because fed by its gifts. This re-entrance into our Origin and acceptance of our true inheritance is the spiritual life of prayer, as it may be experienced by the human soul. Far better to be a shrimp within that ocean, than a full-sized theological whale cast upon the shore.

The Golden Sequence

Fifth Sunday in Lent—
Passion Sunday

CROSS AND SACRAMENT

To look at the Crucifix—'the supreme symbol of our august religion'—and then to look at our own hearts; to test by the Cross the quality of our love—if we do that honestly and unflinchingly we don't need any other self-examination than that, any other judgement or purgation. The lash, the crown of thorns, the mockery, the stripping, the nails—life has equivalents of all these for us and God asks a love for Himself and His children which can accept and survive all that in the particular way in which it is offered to us. It is no use to talk in a large vague way about the love of God; *here* is its point of insertion in the world of men.

What about the dreadful moment when a great test of courage, great suffering, a great bereavement faced us and we knew we were for it and found the agony was more than we could face? The revelation that someone we trusted could not be trusted any more, that someone loved profit better than they loved us? How do we feel when we have to suffer for someone else's wrongdoing? How do we bear mockery and contempt, especially if it is directed at our religious life or at the unfortunate discrepancy between our religious life and our character? What about the sting, the lash, or humiliation or disappointment, the unfortunate events that stripped us of the seamless drapery of self-respect and convention and left us naked to the world; the wounds given by those we loved best; the loneliness inseparable from some phase of the spiritual life? All this happens over and over again. Can we weave it all into the sacrifice of love? . . .

There is a type of ancient picture which shows all the Sacraments centred in and dependent from the Cross: the love self-given there giving itself forever to men, the undying source of grace and purification and truth. It is a wonderful image of what the Christian Church and Christian life really are, a continuation of the Incarnation. It reminds us that the Spirit of Christ is now living and truly present with and in His Church, His Family, His Mystic Body, and, because of His one eternal sacrifice ever giving us His life, and that we are utterly and entirely dependent on that life as branches on the Vine, His touch still cleansing us, His hand still feeding us. Either secretly or sacramentally all living Christians are perpetual penitents and perpetual communicants, there is no other way of carrying on. The Eucharist represents a perpetual pouring out of His very life to feed and enhance our small and feeble lives. Think only of that as we kneel before the window of His Passion and a wonderful joy and gratitude tempers our shame.

Light of Christ

Monday of the Fifth Week in Lent

THE KINGDOM

IT is a great thing for any soul to say without reserve in respect of its own life, 'Thy Kingdom come!' for this means not only the acknowledgement of our present alienation, our fundamental egoism and impurity, but the casting down of the will, the destruction of our small natural sovereignty; the risk and adventure which accompany an unconditional submission to God, a total acceptance of the rule of love. None can guess beforehand with what anguish, what tearing of old hard tissues and habits, the Kingdom will force a path into the soul, and confront self-love in its last fortress with the penetrating demand of God. Yet we cannot use the words unless we are prepared to pay this price: nor is the prayer of adoration real, unless it leads on to this. When we said, 'Hallowed be Thy Name!' we acknowledged the priority of Holiness. Now we offer ourselves for the purposes of Holiness: handing ourselves over to God that His purposes, great or small, declared or secret, natural or spiritual, may be fulfilled through us and in us, and all that is hostile to His Kingdom done away.

There will be two sides to this: passive and active. The passive side means enduring, indeed welcoming, the inexorable pressure of God's transforming power in our own lives; for the Kingdom comes upon earth bit by bit, as first one soul and then another is subjugated by love and so redeemed. It means enduring the burning glance of the Holy, where that glance falls on imperfection, hardness, sin. The active side means a self-offering for the purposes of the Kingdom, here and now in this visible world of space and time; the whole drive of our life, all our natural endowments, set towards a furtherance of the purposes of God. Those purposes will not be fulfilled till the twist has been taken out of experience, and everything on earth conforms to the pattern in heaven—that is to say, in the Mind of God: widespreading love transfiguring the whole texture of life. Here we have a direct responsibility as regards our whole use of created things: money, time, position, the politics we support, the papers we read. It is true that the most drastic social reform, the most complete dethronement of privilege, cannot of themselves bring the Kingdom in; for peace and joy in the Holy Spirit can only come to us by the free gift of the Transcendent. But at least these can clear ground, prepare the highway of God; and here each act of love, each sacrifice, each conquest of prejudice, each generous impulse carried through into action counts: and each unloving gesture, hard judgement, pessimistic thought or utterance opposes the coming of the Kingdom and falsifies the life of prayer.

Light of Christ

Tuesday of the Fifth Week in Lent

FOOD

THE symbolism of food plays a large part in all religions, and especially in Christianity. As within the mysteries of the created order we must all take food and give food—more, must take life and give life—we are here already in touch with the 'life-giving and terrible mysteries of Christ,' who indwells that order; for all is the sacramental expression of His all-demanding and all-giving life. We accept our constant dependence on physical food as a natural and inevitable thing. Yet it is not necessarily so: there are creatures which are free from it for very long periods of time. But perhaps because of his border-line status, his embryonic capacity for God, man is kept in constant memory of his own fragility, unable to maintain his existence for long without food from beyond himself; his bodily life dependent on the humble plants and animals that surround him, his soul's life on the unfailing nourishment of the life of God. 'I am the Bread of Life that came down from heaven. He that eateth of *this* bread shall live for ever.' Eternal life is the gift, the self-imparting of the Eternal God. We cannot claim it in our own right.

The Biblical writers make plain to us how easily and inevitably men have given spiritual rank to this primitive truth of life's dependence on food, and seen in it the image of a deeper truth which concerns the very ground of our being. . . .

Throughout His ministry, our Lord emphasized the idea of feeding as something intimately connected with His love and care for souls. The mystery of the Eucharist does not stand alone. It is the crest of a great wave; a total sacramental disclosure of

80

the dealings of the Transcendent God with men. The hunger of the four thousand and five thousand are more than miracles of practical compassion; we feel that in them something of deep significance is done, one of the mysteries of Eternal Life a little bit unveiled. So too in the Supper at Emmaus, when the bread is broken the Holy One is known. It is peculiar to Christianity, indeed part of the mystery of the Incarnation, that it constantly shows us this coming of God through and in homely and fugitive things and events; and puts the need and dependence of the creature at the very heart of prayer.

Abba

Wednesday of the Fifth Week in Lent

LOVE, JOY, PEACE

'THE fruit of the Spirit,' says St. Paul, 'is Love, Joy, Peace, Long-suffering, Gentleness, Goodness, Faithfulness, Meekness, Temperance'—all the things the world most needs. A clear issue, is it not? To discover the health and reality of our life of prayer, we need not analyse it or fuss about it. But we must consider whether it tends, or does not tend, to produce just these fruits, because they are the necessary results of the action of God in the soul. These are the fruits of human nature when it has opened itself to the action of the Eternal Love: what the 'new creature in Christ' (which if we are really Christians, we are all in process of becoming) is to be like. So they are very good subjects for meditation. A good gardener always has an idea of what he is trying to grow; without vision even a cabbage patch will perish. . . .

I do not think that Saint Paul arranged his list of the fruits of the Spirit in a casual order. They represent a progressive series from one point and that one point is Love, the living, eternal seed from which all grow. We all know that Christians are baptized 'into a life summed up in love,' even though we have to spend the rest of our own lives learning how to do it. Love therefore is the budding point from which all the rest come: that tender, cherishing attitude; that unlimited self-forgetfulness, generosity and kindness which is the attitude of God to all His creatures and so must be the attitude towards them which His Spirit brings forth in us. If that is frost-bitten we need not hope for any of the rest. 'Whoso dwelleth in Charity dwelleth in

God and God in him.' To be unloving is to be out of touch with God. . . .

The Fruit of the Spirit is Love, Joy, Peace—that threefold formula of blessedness.

First comes Love, Charity; pure, undemanding, generous love of God in Himself and of His creatures, good and bad, congenial and uncongenial, for His sake; a certain share in His generous, loving action, the way He cares for all life. Each Christian soul who learns that in prayer and teaches it in every-day life, has made a contribution to the peace of the world. He who loveth not knoweth not God. In hard, ungenerous hearts, the Spirit cannot grow and increase. We can understand that bit even though we cannot always practise it. But then Saint Paul suddenly ascends to the very summit of the spirit and says, not that the spirit of love shall bring forth such suitable qualities as penitence, diligence, helpfulness, unworldliness, good social and religious habits, but that the real sign that God the Giver of Life, has been received into our souls will be joy and peace: joy, the spirit of selfless delight; peace, the spirit of tranquil acceptance; the very character of the beatitude of Heaven, given here and *now* in our grubby little souls, provided only that they are loving little souls. If, in spite of all conflicts, weakness, sufferings, sins, we open our door, the spirit is poured out within us and the first mark of its presence is not an increase of energy but joy and peace.

We should not have guessed that. Yet real love always heals fear and neutralizes egotism, and so, as love grows up in us, we shall worry about ourselves less and less, and admire and delight in God and His other children more and more, and this is the secret of joy. We shall no longer strive for our own way, but commit ourselves, easily and simply, to God's way, acquiesce in His will and in so doing find our peace. And bit by bit there grows up in us a quiet but ardent spiritual life, tending to God, adoring God, resting in God. Peace and joy are necessarily permanent characteristics of true spiritual life, the signs of God's abiding presence in the soul. They are not something we achieve at the *end*, but are there at the very beginning, in our soul's deeps, long indeed before our restless surface-minds are ready to receive them. 'He shall have peace whose mind is stayed on Thee.'

The Fruits of the Spirit

Thursday of the Fifth Week in Lent

LONG-SUFFERING, GENTLENESS

THE next fruit of the Spirit, says Saint Paul, is long-suffering and gentleness—much patient endurance as regards what life does to us, much loving-kindness, care, consideration in all contacts with other lives. Here another region is submitted to God's influence and in consequence another source of strain taken away. If the first three fruits form a little group growing up at the soul's very centre, gentleness and long-suffering are borne on the branches that stretch out towards the world. They are the earnest of what Ruysbroeck calls the wide-spreading nature of love, giving itself to all in common, kind to the unjust as well as the just.

Consider first the long-suffering of God, the long-suffering and gentleness of Absolute Perfection and Absolute Power, and how the further we press into the deeps of spiritual experience, the more those qualities are seen. How God looks past the imperfections of men (as we look past those of children), with what unexacting love He accepts and uses the faulty. See how Christ deliberately chooses Peter; while completely realizing Peter, his unreliable qualities, his boasting and cocksureness, his prompt capitulation to fear. Peter's family must have thought, 'Thank Heaven! a chance for the tiresome creature now' when he joined the apostolic band. But Christ did not just put up with him. He offered him a continual and special friendship, knowing what was in the man. He took Peter into the inner fastness of Gethesemane and asked for his prayer and did not get it. (Is that the way we handle our tiresome and unreliable friends? Because it is with personal contacts we have always got to begin.) It was to Peter Christ addressed His rare reproach, 'What! Could you not watch one hour?' and it was from this that Peter went to the denial. Yet in spite of all, the long-suffering love and trust of Christ won in the end and made Peter the chief of the Apostles—the Rock—what irony!—on which He built the Church. He was right, for here the Church is now. In Peter's care and to Peter's love Christ left the feeding of the sheep: a remarkable sequel. Who shines in that series of events? Christ or Peter? Christ shines—but Peter is transformed. Christ's attitude and action are only possible to holiness and they are justified by results. Here is a standard set for us in our dealings with the faulty. The fruit of the Spirit is never rigorism but always long-suffering. No startling high standard. No all or nothing demands. But gentleness and tolerance in spiritual, moral, emotional, intellectual judgements and claims.

The Fruits of the Spirit

Friday of the Fifth Week in Lent

GOODNESS, FAITHFULNESS

THIS time we have two quite positive qualities. If on one hand the Spirit brings forth a quiet and patient acquiescence in God's purpose, on the other hand it brings forth a quality of personal fitness for His service. Goodness, of course, does not merely bear our cheap modern meanings of either goodness or pleasantness; the 'good woman' or the 'good fellow.' It has no special reference to correct moral behaviour. It is a word that denotes perfection of quality: a good run, good cheese, good vintage, good stuff, good garden soil—the opposite number to every kind of imperfection, shoddiness and cheapness. The fruit of God's presence and action in the soul is an enhancement of our quality. It is better stuff right through than it was before. The Greek word carries with it a certain character of perfection, nobility, rightness, even beauty. The Good Shepherd is not just the very kind, devoted, attentive, conscientious shepherd: He is the classic pattern of all shepherds, had a total quality of beauty and completeness. . . .

Faithfulness is consecration in overalls. It is the steady acceptance and performance of the common duty and immediate task without any reference to personal preferences—because it is there to be done and so is a manifestation of the Will of God. It is Elizabeth Leseur settling down each day to do the household accounts quite perfectly (when she would much rather have been in church) and saying 'the duties of my station come before everything else.' It is Brother Lawrence taking his turn in the kitchen, and Saint Francis de Sales taking the burden of a difficult diocese and saying, 'I have now little time for prayer—but I do what is the same.'

The fruits of the Spirit get less and less showy as we go on. Faithfulness means continuing quietly with the job we have been given, in the situation where we have been placed; not yielding to the restless desire for change. It means tending the lamp quietly for God without wondering how much longer it has got to go on. Steady, unsensational driving, taking good care of the car. A lot of the road to heaven has to be taken at thirty miles per hour. . . .

The first step taken towards Calvary was the worst: but in the first step all was achieved. Be thou faithful unto death—and I will give thee the Crown of Life. Faithfulness is one of the sturdy qualities most dear to the heart of God. Peter was offered just the same chance of the same royal virtue. Jesus was victorious on the Cross. Peter was defeated, warming himself by the fire, for the night was cold. I wonder how *we* should act if the same sort of crisis, charged with fear and quite devoid of consolation, came our way? It is a crisis which in some form all the saints have had to face.

You remember the noble figure of Faithful in the *Pilgrim's Progress*, Christian's best friend. How he started from the City of Destruction some time after Christian, but soon passed him on the road because he never thought it necessary to linger, to ask for help or explanations in the House of the Interpreter, or worry about dangers in the way. He just plodded steadily on. Christian, who is the sort of excellent man who gets full value out of all obstacles, worries constantly and leaves nothing to chance; he is surprised to find how well Faithful has got on and says, 'But what about the lions in the path?' Faithful said he had never noticed any lions, he thought they must have been having their after-dinner snooze. And when he got to the Valley of Humiliation, he *was* attacked by two temptations, one to shame and one to discontent, but made short work of both. After that he went all the way in sunshine through the

Valley of Humiliation and the terrible Valley of the Shadow of Death.

That, I think, is one of Bunyan's loveliest bits. Faithful is the least self-occupied of all the pilgrims. We hear nothing about his burden or fatigue or difficulty or the poor state of the road. Christian makes a good deal of the Valley of Humiliation, tells us about how horrible it was and feels it very remarkable that he ever got through the Valley of the Shadow of Death. There is none of that in Faithful. He is not thinking about saving his soul. He is thinking about God. And so he goes in sunshine all the way.

The Fruits of the Spirit

Saturday of the Fifth Week in Lent

MEEKNESS, TEMPERANCE

'THOUGH I give my body to be burned,' said Saint Paul, 'and have not love, I am nothing.' I do not as a supernatural being exist. And now he gives us another and much more surprising test of spiritual vitality. Though you feel an unconquerable love, joy and peace, though you are gentle, long-suffering, good in all your personal relationships, though you are utterly faithful in your service of God—in the end the only proof that all this is truly the fruit of the Spirit, Christ in you and not just your own idea, is the presence of the last two berries on the bunch: not showy berries, not prominently placed, but absolutely decisive for the classification of the plant. Meekness and Temperance, says the Authorized Version or, as we may quite properly translate, Humility and Moderation. That means our possession of the crowning grace of creatureliness: knowing our own size and own place, the self-oblivion and quietness with which we fit into God's great scheme instead of having a jolly little scheme of our own, and are content to bring forth the fruit of His Spirit, according to our own measure, here and now in space and time.

Humility and Moderation—the graces of the self-forgetful soul—we might almost expect that if we have grasped all that the Incarnation really means—God and His love, manifest not in some peculiar and supernatural spiritual manner, but in ordinary human nature. Christ, first-born of many brethren, content to be one of us, living the family life and from within His Church inviting the souls of men to share His family life.

In the family circle there is room for the childish and the imperfect and the naughty, but the uppish is always out of place.

We have got down to the bottom of the stairs now and are fairly sitting on the mat. But the proof that it is the right flight and leads up to the Divine Charity, is the radiance that pours down from the Upper story: the joy and peace in which the whole is bathed and which floods our whole being here in the lowest place. How right Saint Paul was to put these two fruits at the end of his list, for as a rule they are the last we acquire. At first we simply do not see the point. But the saints have always seen it. When Angela of Foligno was dying, her disciples asked for a last message and she, who had been called a Mistress in Theology and whose Visions of the Being of God are among the greatest the medieval mystics have left us, had only one thing to say to them as her farewell: 'Make yourselves small! Make yourselves very small.'

The Fruits of the Spirit

Palm Sunday

CROSS AND CHURCH

In his letter to the Romans, we find Saint Paul asking his converts if they realize what it means to be part of the Church. It means, he says (and we can imagine their surprise when they heard it), being received into the death of Christ—the unconditional sacrifice of the Cross—in order to walk in newness of life: transformed through self-loss into a bit of that Body which is indwelt and ruled by the Spirit of Divine Charity. No easy application for membership, then, fulfils the demands of real Christianity. It is a crisis, a radical choice, a deep and costly change. When we judge our own lives by this standard we realize that full entrance into the Church's real life must for most of us be a matter of growth. There are layers of our minds, both personal and corporate, still untransformed; not indwelt by Charity, resisting the action of God. There are many things the Spirit could do through us, for the healing and redeeming of the world, if it were not for our cowardice, slackness, fastidiousness, or self-centred concentration on our own jobs.

'Present yourselves to God as alive from the dead,' says Saint Paul; and your members—all you have, every bit of you— as instruments, tools of righteousness. That is his standard of Churchmanship. That is the kind of life into which he conceives his converts are baptized; and there is something desperately vigorous and definite about it. What he seems to envisage in the Church is a vast distributing system of the Divine Charity. As we were slaves of 'sin'—that is, held tight in a life which is alien from the real purposes of God, off the track, and uses its great energies for its own ends—so, that taking a new direction which is involved in becoming a Christian, means the turning over of all that energy to God's purposes; using it for Him, co-operating with the Spirit working within life for the redemption and hallowing of the whole world. That is what the Church is for; and the Sacraments are there to help those who are prepared to pull their weight.

The School of Charity

Monday in Holy Week

ABASEMENT AND ADOPTION

HIS Spirit comes to us, as Caussade said, in 'the sacrament of the present moment.' Joy and pain, drudgery and delight, humiliation and consolation, tension and peace—each of these contrasting experiences reaches us fully charged with God; and does, or should incite us to an ever more complete self-giving to God. But each experience, as such, is neutral when seen only in natural regard. It is then merely part of that endless chain of cause and effect of which our temporal lives are made. It can only touch our deepest selves, help or hinder the growth of the spirit, in so far as we do or do not direct our wills through it in love and reverence to Him. There is only one life—the 'spiritual' life consists in laying hold on it in a particular way; so that action becomes charged with contemplation, and the Infinite is served in and through all finite things. The twofold experience of Spirit, as a deeply felt inward Presence and as the Ocean of reality and life, must be actualized in a twofold response of the soul: a response which is at once 'active' and 'contemplative,' outgoing and indrawing, an adoring gaze on the Splendour over against us, and a humble loving movement towards the surrendered union of will and Will. . . .

Thus total abasement before the transcendent Perfect is one side of the spiritual life. Adoption into the supernatural series—divine sonship, with its obligation of faithful service within the Divine order—is the other side. The Seraphim in Isaiah's vision, who veiled their faces before the unmeasured Glory, were yet part of the economy through which that Glory was poured out on the world: and the experience of reality which begins with the prophet's awestruck vision and utter abasement before the Holy, ends on the words 'Send me'!

The double action of the soul, standing away from the Perfect in contemplation and seeking union with It in love, and this double consciousness of the Holy as both our Home and our Father, are the characters of a fully developed Christian spirituality. But these characters are not found in their classic completeness in any one individual. We only discern their balanced splendour in the corporate life of surrendered spirits; the Communion of Saints. Not the individual mystic in his solitude, but the whole of that Mystical Body, in its ceaseless self-offering to God, is the unit of humanity in which we can find reflected the pattern of the spiritual life. And as regards to the individual, the very essence of that life is contained in a docile acceptance of his own peculiar limitations and capacities, a loyal response to vocation—a response which, though it may sometimes be passive in appearance, is ever charged with the activity of God. 'I see no difference,' said Bérulle, as he bade farewell to his brethren before setting forth upon an onerous mission, 'between those who go and those who stay at home. In one sense all are sent; for there is a double mission, one interior and the other exterior. And it is on the interior mission of grace, of mercy, and of charity, that I declare all to be sent.'

The Golden Sequence

Tuesday in Holy Week

FORGIVENESS

THERE is no lesson Christ loves better to drive home, than this disconcerting fact of our common human fragility: which, when we have truly grasped it, kills resentment and puts indulgent pity in its place. Let the man, the group, the nation that is without sin cast the first stone. God's forgiveness means the compassionate recognition of the weakness and instability of man; how often we cannot help it, how truly there is in us a 'root and ground of sin,' an implicit rebellion against the Holy, a tendency away from love and peace. And this requires of us the constant compassionate recognition of our fellow-creatures' instability and weakness; of the fact that they too cannot help it. If the Christian penitent dares to ask that his many departures from the Christian norm, his impatience, gloom, self-occupation, unloving prejudices, reckless tongue, feverish desires, with all the damage they have caused to Christ's Body, are indeed to be set aside, because—in spite of all—he longs for God and Eternal Life; then he too must set aside and forgive all that impatience, selfishness, bitter and foolish speech, sudden yieldings to base impulse in others have caused him to endure. Hardness is the one impossible thing. Harshness to others in those who ask and need the mercy of God sets up a conflict at the very heart of personality and shuts the door upon grace. And that which is true of the individual soul, is also true of the community; the penitent nation seeking the path of life must also conform to the law of charity.

This principle applied in its fullness makes a demand on our generosity which only a purified and self-oblivious love can hope to meet. For every soul that appeals for God's forgiveness is required to move over to His side, and share the compassionate understanding, the unmeasured pity, with which He looks on human frailty and sin. So difficult is this to the proud and assertive creature, that it comes very near the end of our education in prayer. Indeed, the Christian doctrine of forgiveness is so drastic and so difficult, where there is a real and deep injury to forgive, that only those living in the Spirit, in union with the Cross, can dare to base their claim on it.

Abba

Wednesday in Holy Week

UNION WITH GOD

ALL gardeners know the importance of good root development before we force the leaves and flowers. So our life in God should be deeply rooted and grounded before we presume to expect to produce flowers and fruits; otherwise we risk shooting up into one of those lanky plants which can never do without a stick. We are constantly beset by the notion that we ought to perceive ourselves springing up quickly, like the seed on stony ground; show striking signs of spiritual growth. But perhaps we are only required to go on quietly, making root, growing nice and bushy; docile to the great slow rhythm of life. When we see no startling marks of our own religious progress or our usefulness to God, it is well to remember the baby in the stable and the little boy in the streets of Nazareth. The very life was there present, which was to change the whole history of the human race, the rescuing action of God. At that stage there was not much to show for it; yet there is perfect continuity between the stable and the Easter garden, and the thread that unites them is the hidden Will of God. The childish prayer of Nazareth was the right preparation for the awful prayer of the Cross.

So it is that the life of the Spirit is to unfold gently and steadily within us; till at the last the full stature for which God designed us is attained. It is an organic process, a continuous Divine action; not a sudden miracle or a series of jerks. Therefore there should be no struggle, impatience, self-willed effort in our prayer and self-discipline; but rather a great flexibility, a homely ordered life, a gentle acceptance of what comes to us, and a still gentler acceptance of the fact that much we see in others is still out of our own reach. The prayer of the growing spirit should be free, humble, simple; full of confidence and full of initiative too.

The mystics constantly tell us, that the goal of this prayer and of the hidden life which shall itself become more and more of a prayer, is union with God. We meet this phrase often: far too often, for we lose the wholesome sense of its awfulness. What does union with God mean? Not a nice feeling which we enjoy in devout movements. This may or may not be a by-product of union with God; probably not. It can never be its substance. Union with God means such an entire self-giving to the Divine Charity, such identification with its interests, that the whole of our human nature is transformed in God, irradiated by His absolute light, His sanctifying grace. Thus it is woven up into the organ of His creative activity, His redeeming purpose; conformed to the pattern of Christ, heart, soul, mind and strength. Each time this happens, it means that one more creature has achieved its destiny; and each soul in whom the life of the spirit is born, sets out towards that goal.

The School of Charity

Maundy Thursday

INCARNATION AND EUCHARIST

FOR the fully Christian life is a Eucharistic life: that is, a natural life conformed to the pattern of Jesus, given in its wholeness to God, laid on His altar as a sacrifice of love, and consecrated, transformed by His inpouring life, to be used to give life and food to other souls. It will be, according to its measure and special call, adoring, declaratory, intercessory and redemptive: but always a vehicle of the Supernatural. The creative spirit of God is a redemptive and cherishing love; and it is as friends and fellow workers with the Spirit, tools of the Divine redemptive action that Christians are required to live. 'You are the Body of Christ,' said Saint Augustine to his communicants. That is to say, in you and through you the method and work of the Incarnation must go forward. You are meant to incarnate in your lives the theme of your adoration. You are to be taken, consecrated, broken and made means of grace; vehicles of the Eternal Charity.

Thus every Christian communicant volunteers for translation into the supernatural order, and is self-offered for the supernatural purposes of God. The Liturgy leads us out towards Eternity, by way of the acts in which men express their need of God and relation to God. It commits every worshipper to the adventure of holiness, and has no meaning apart from this. In it the Church shows forth again and again her great objective; the hallowing of the whole created order and the restoration of all things in Christ. The Liturgy recapitulates all the essentials in this life of sanctification—to repent, to pray, to listen, to learn; and then to offer upon the altar of God, to intercede, to be transformed to the purposes of God, to be fed and maintained by the very life of God. And though it is the voice of the Church, none the less in it is to be recognized the voice of each separate soul, and the care of the Praying Church for each separate soul. 'Holy Things for the Holy!' cries the celebrant in the earliest liturgies, as he lifts up the consecrated gifts. Not 'Good Things for the Good'; but supernatural things for those imperfect creatures who have been baptized into the Supernatural, translated to another order—those looking towards God the Perfect and beginning to conceive of life as a response to God the Perfect; but unable without the 'rich bread of Christ' to actualize the state to which they are called.

The Mystery of Sacrifice

Good Friday

THE CROSS AND ITS DEMANDS

'It is not the act of a good disciple,' says Saint John of the Cross, 'to flee from the Cross in order to enjoy the sweetness of an easy piety.' So here above all, by the Crucifix and what it means to us, we test the quality of our discipleship. What we think about the Cross means ultimately what we think about life, for 'seek where you will,' says à Kempis, 'everywhere you will find the Cross.' And when you have found it, what are you going to do about it? That is the question: look at it with horror or with adoration?

It has been said that the whole life of Christ was a Cross. I think that saying does grave injustice to its richness of response, to the real expansion and joy and beauty of His contacts with nature, children, friends; the true happiness we find again in the saints nearest to Him; the hours snatched for the deep joy of prayer and communion; the outburst of rejoicing when He discerns the Father's Will. But it was the deep happiness of the entirely self-abandoned, not the easy shallow satisfaction of those who live to express themselves and enjoy themselves; that Perfect Joy which Saint Francis rediscovered in abjection; and which was ratified on La Verna when he was caught into the supernatural order and sealed with the wounds of Christ.

There is a marked contrast between the first phase of the Ministry with its confident movement within the natural world; mending what is wrong with it, using what is right in it and sharing the social life of men, and that after the Transfiguration, the second phase, with its sense of a deepening conflict with that easy, happy world; the conviction that what is deeply wrong with it can only be mended by sacrifice; that the Suffering Servant is the one who serves His brethren best. 'Take up the

Cross if you wish to follow Me!' The spiritually natural life is charming, but it stops short of all that God asks of the really surrendered soul.

It was in the Passion, says Saint John of the Cross, that Christ 'finished that supreme work which His whole life, its miracles and works of power, had not accomplished: the union and reconciliation of human nature with the life of God.' Here we learn all that it means to acknowledge Him as our Way, our Truth and our Life. I suppose no soul of any sensitiveness can live through Holy Week without an awed and grateful sense of being incorporated in a mystery of self-giving love which yet remains far beyond our span.

Light of Christ

Easter Even

THE RESURRECTION FAITH

I AM writing to you at the moment in the Christian year when, as it were, we pause and look back on the richest cluster of such spiritual facts ever revealed to man. Paschal Time, to give its old name to the interval between Easter and Ascension, marks the end of the historical manifestation of the Word Incarnate, and the beginning of His hidden life within the Church. But the quality of that hidden life, in which as members of the Body of Christ we are all required to take part, is the quality which the historic life revealed. From the very beginning the Church has been sure that the series of events which were worked out to their inevitable end in Holy Week sum up and express the deepest secrets of the relation of God to men.

That means, of course, that Christianity can never be merely a pleasant or consoling religion. It is a stern business. It is concerned with the salvation through sacrifice and love of a world in which, as we can all see now, evil and cruelty are rampant. Its supreme symbol is the Crucifix—the total and loving self-giving of man to the redeeming purposes of God.

Because we are all the children of God we all have our part to play in His redemptive plan; and the Church consists of those loving souls who have accepted this obligation, with all that it costs. Its members are all required to live, each in their own way, through the sufferings and self-abandonment of the Cross; as the only real contribution which they can make to the redemption of the world. Christians, like their Master, must be ready to accept the worst that evil and cruelty can do to them, and vanquish it by the power of love.

For if sacrifice, total self-giving to God's mysterious purpose, is what is asked of us, His answer to that sacrifice is the gift of power. Easter and Whitsuntide complete the Christian Mystery by showing us first our Lord Himself and then His chosen apostles possessed of a new power—the power of the Spirit—which changed every situation in which they were placed. That supernatural power is still the inheritance of every Christian and our idea of Christianity is distorted and incomplete unless we rely on it. It is this power and only this which can bring in the new Christian society of which we hear so much. We ought to pray for it; expect it and trust it; and as we do this, we shall gradually become more and more sure of it.

'Letter to the Prayer Group, Eastertide, 1941,' *The Fruits of the Spirit*